ONCE UPON A PINT

TO CAROL

For in every sense, it is her book, too.

ONCE UPON A PINT

A Reader's Guide to the
Literary Pubs & Inns of

DORSET &
SOMERSET

Terry Townsend

PiXZ

First published in Great Britain in 2013

Copyright © Terry Townsend 2013

British Library Cataloguing-in-Publication Data
A CIP record for this title is available from the British Library

ISBN 978 0 85704 215 6

PiXZ Books
Halsgrove House, Ryelands Business Park,
Bagley Road, Wellington, Somerset TA21 9PZ
Tel: 01823 653777
Fax: 01823 216796
email: sales@halsgrove.com

An imprint of Halstar Ltd, part of the
Halsgrove group of companies
Information on all Halsgrove titles is
available at: www.halsgrove.com

Printed and bound in China by
Everbest Printing Co Ltd

CONTENTS

INTRODUCTION

On 21 March, 1776, Dr Johnson told his biographer James Boswell that: 'There is nothing which has yet been contrived by man, by which so much happiness is produced as by a good tavern or inn'. Hang on a minute Dr J; surely you're forgetting something? What about a good book? Most people derive happiness from a good book long before they ever enter a tavern or inn.

Luckily we don't need to debate the question because it is not an either/or situation – we can have both! Indeed, English Literature and English inns have been inseparable since the time Chaucer left the Tabard Inn in 1372 with his band of pilgrims bound for Canterbury. The host of the Tabard, Harry Bailly, elected to travel with them and offered the prize of a feast on their return for the pilgrim who told the best tale.

When one initially thinks of 'Literary Pubs', Charles Dickens might be the name that comes to mind and the peregrinations of Mr Pickwick. But, to this day, writers of all types continue to use pubs as a convenient means of bringing characters together; just look at 'The Rover's Return' and 'The Queen Vic' on Albert Square.

Whether it is known as an inn, an alehouse, a tavern or even a hotel bar, matters little; the distinctions have always been blurred. What is important is that, at its best, a good pub can be an oasis offering warmth, friendship, jokes and philosophy – much like a good book.

Most people enjoy visiting old inns simply because they feel a vague sense of history. This pleasure can be greatly enhanced if a few facts are known about its past. And there are often less tangible things that can foster a feeling of human attachment and belonging; like knowing you are in a special place that inspired a writer to create a scene of love, drama, intrigue or comedy.

Every county in England has its share of literary pubs and inns but the southern counties are particularly blessed. This book is a literary pub crawl around two of England's most beautiful and least spoilt shires; following in the steps of famous and lesser known writers. Researching the background provided me with the great enjoyment of discovering books that I would not otherwise have read and journeying to places that I would not otherwise have seen. I hope the same might be true for you.

Here are town pubs, country pubs, village pubs, riverside pubs and seaside pubs all with one thing in common; they have been immortalised by association with books or writers. Among the many other characters you will meet along the way are Lorna Doone, Sam Weller, Inspector Morse, Tess of the d'Urbervilles, Barry Lyndon, The Ancient Mariner, Anne Elliot and her Captain Wentworth, The French Lieutenant's

Woman, The Mayor of Casterbridge and a Poet Laureate turned thriller writer.

I have not attempted to report on the facilities on offer in respect of the beer, food or accommodation because these things change and there is always plenty of good up-to-date information available. One source I have always found reliable is *The Good Pub Guide* edited by Alisdair Aird and Fiona Stapley.

The literary pilgrimage has long been accepted as a good excuse to travel. Now, if you need it, you have a good excuse to pop down the pub. Cheers and good reading.

r. Henchard," whispered Mrs. Newson who, since her entry into Caster
ridge, had seemed strangely weak and agitated, "And this, I think, woul
e a good place for trying it--just to ask, you know, how he stands in th
own--if he is here, as I think he must be. You, Elizabeth-Jane, had better b
he one to do it. I'm too worn out to do anything--pull down your fall first
She sat down upon the lowest step, and Elizabeth-Jane obeyed he
irections and stood among the idlers.

"What's going on to-night?" asked the girl, after singling out an old ma
nd standing by him long enough to acquire a neighbourly right o
onverse.

"Well, ye must be a stranger sure," said the old man, without taking h
yes from the window. "Why, 'tis a great dinner of the gentle-peop
nd such like leading volk--wi the Mayor in the chair. As we plainer fellov
ain't invited, they leave the winder-shutters open that we may get jist
ense o't out here. If you mount the steps you can see em. That's M
lenchard, the Mayor, at the end of the table, a facing ye; and that's th
ouncil men right and left....Ah, lots of them when they begun life wei
o more than I be now!"

"Henchard!" said Elizabeth-Jane, surprised, but by no means suspectin
he whole force of the revelation. She ascended to the top of the steps.

Her mother, though her head was bowed, had already caught from th
an-window tones that strangely riveted her attention, before the ol
nan's words, "Mr. Henchard, the Mayor," reached her ears. She aros
nd stepped up to her daughter's side as soon as she could do so withou
howing exceptional eagerness.

The interior of the hotel dining-room was spread out before her, wit
s tables, and glass, and plate, and inmates. Facing the window, in th
hair of dignity, sat a man about forty years of age; of heavy frame, larg
eatures, and commanding voice; his general build being rather coars
han compact. He had a rich complexion, which verged on swarthiness,
lashing black eye, and dark, bushy brows and hair. When he indulged i
n occasional loud laugh at some remark among the guests, his larg
nouth parted so far back as to show to the rays of the chandelier a fu
core or more of the two-and-thirty sound white teeth that he obvious
ill could boast of.

11

The Rose & Crown, Bradford Abbas appears as The Farmer's Rest, King's Barton in John Cowper Powys' 1929 novel *Wolf Solent*.

BRADFORD ABBAS

Rose & Crown

John Cowper Powys (1872 - 1963)

The carved stone mantle beam over the fireplace in the bar was revealed during refurbishment work. It is thought to have come from either Sherborne Abbey or nearby Maybank House.

In John Cowper Powys' 1929 novel *Wolf Solent* the North Dorset village of Bradford Abbas appears as King's Barton and the Rose & Crown village pub as The Farmer's Rest.

Bradford Abbas is located a little South off the A30 between Yeovil, which appears as Black Sod and the small attractive Abbey town of Sherborne, which features as Ramsgard.

The area was well known to Powys from the time of his childhood, as his father had been curate of the church which stands next to the pub – and

The walls of the bar are decorated with photographs of local characters including this wonderful image which is headed 'Lads from the Village 1934'. These former regulars are: George Chainey (87), James Higgins (87), Samuel Ring (90), Thomas Coombs (89) and Sidney Parsons (81) – combined ages 434 years!

The Eldridge Pope lantern is a reminder of the former Dorchester brewers. Their strong beer 'brisk as a volcano; piquant, yet without a twang' was a favourite of Thomas Hardy and he eulogised it In *The Trumpet Major*.

a master at Sherborne School, which his son had attended.

This, the first and most cohesive of Powys' four great Wessex novels, was a particularly remarkable achievement. It was written in hotel rooms and trains across America; towards the end of a debilitating series of lecture tours undertaken by the author.

After ten years in London Wolf Solent, the young hero of the novel, returns to Dorset to work as a literary assistant to one John Urqhart. The story is complex, humorous, romantic and sometimes extravagant; written with extraordinary vitality and memorable beauty.

The Rose & Crown is the quintessential village pub with four linked rooms. The charming sheltered garden is overlooked by the medieval church. In fact, both buildings occupy a central place in the geography of the village and of the novel as rumours emanate from the tap room of The Farmer's Rest concerning the fate of Urqhart's assistant Redfern who is buried in the churchyard.

BRIDPORT
Bull Hotel

Thomas Hardy (1840 - 1928)

Thomas Hardy's short story *Fellow Townsmen* is set here in Bridport. One of the townsmen is George Barnet, a gentleman of means inherited from his family's connection with the local rope-making industry.

The old town is Hardy's Port Bredy which consists mainly of two principal streets. Hardy's Black-Bull Hotel is located in the long, wide main street running down hill, east-west. The harbour road, intersects the high street at a T-junction by the Market House and heads due south for a mile and a half down to West Bay on Dorset's Jurassic coast. This road and the harbour feature significantly in the story.

The Bull Hotel, located in the long, wide main street of Bridport, appears as The Black Bull Hotel, Port Bredy in Thomas Hardy's short story *Fellow Townsmen.*

At one time the Bull was one of the most famous coaching inns in the West Country and is one of those resilient, old fashioned hostelries that have somehow survived more than 500 years of England's turbulent history. The sixteenth-century inn has a striking, blue-painted stuccoed nineteenth-century façade. It stands three storeys high with prominent bay

The calm of the Bull's sympathetically restored interior is just a step off the bustling High Street.
Photo courtesy of Heatheronhertravels.com

windows from pavement level and is three or four times the width of any of the adjacent buildings.

Hardy's characters enter and exit the scene via the Bull's stage-coach. When George Barnet loses Lucy (the girl he loves) to his fellow townsman, he departs from the inn to travel abroad for more than twenty-one years. At the close of the story, he arrives back at the hotel where we see him disappearing up the staircase, preceded by a chamber maid with a candle followed by a lad with his trunk. In the final scene, Lucy goes herself to the Bull, and questions the staff closely but (in true Hardy style) Barnet has left without leaving a note.

The Bridport Arms at West Bay is Hardy's Harbour Inn of the story. Built directly on to the beach, this is where George Barnett first considered carrying the apparently lifeless body of his wife, following her drowning.

The Sailor's Return at Chaldon Herring, at the heart of a former colony of writers and artists, has been the subject of a number of books and stories.

CHALDON HERRING
Sailor's Return

T. F. Powys (1875 - 1953)   David Garnett (1892 - 1981)

Between the two World Wars, this tiny village seven miles west of Weymouth, became a Mecca for artists and writers. They were drawn to it not only for its beauty and tranquility but also because it was home to the remarkable author T. F. Powys whose stories explore universal themes within this microcosm of the rural world.

Chaldon Herring features as Folley Down in his haunting novel *Mr Weston's Good Wine*. The title is taken from Jane Austen's *Emma*, in which Mr Weston believes that: 'There is no place in the round world provides more peace and joy to its inhabitants than this village'.

Just up from the village green is the long low whitewashed

Sailor's Return which appropriately enough appears in the story as the Angel, considering that Mr Weston's assistant is the Archangel Michael. The pub, its Landlord Thomas Bunce; 'a gentleman who, by the appearance of him, could be merry in all his parts' and his daughter Jenny are all central to the story.

The Sailor's Return has been enlarged since 1926 but Powys' description (apart from the sign) is still true today:

> *The inn is placed upon a little hill. At its entrance is a finely painted sign board of an angel. The inn itself is covered by a good coating of thatch, that is the very best straw in use in this part of the country and is called reed. The thatch keeps the house warm in winter and cool in summer, and the ale that is kept in a narrow passage between the kitchen and the parlour is by no means in a common way a bad beverage.*

The original cottage bar. The pub has been substantially extended with new wings at both ends.

One of the writers attracted to the village at that time was David Garnett who stayed in the pub and wrote an insightful novel about colour prejudice. The story, published in 1925, is called *The Sailor's Return* and is set in the summer of 1858.

It was the first significant work in British literature to feature a black female as a major character. English sea captain, William Targett, returns to his homeland from a voyage to western Africa and rents a pub in a sleepy Dorset village. Here the former mariner sets about building a life for his African princess bride Tulip and their son Olu, but the local residents and even his own relatives have other ideas. It is a compelling story that, once read, is never forgotten.

CHESIL BEACH, PORTLAND

Cove House Inn

John Cowper Powys (1872 - 1963)

Effectively built in to the sea defenses, the Cove House Inn stands high and defiant against the elements at the Portland end of Chesil Beach, looking as if it might have risen from the waves. This dramatic situation gave J. C. Powys the idea for his fictional name The Sea Serpent's Head which he used in his Wessex novel *Weymouth Sands*.

Powys describes the pub as a:

> *...curious inn... of not more than half-a-dozen rooms all told composed of huge square blocks of Portland stone on the seaward side of the hamlet of Weston...'*

The dramatic situation of Cove House Inn on Chesil Beach gave J. C. Powys the idea for his fictional name The Sea Serpent's Head which he used in his Wessex novel *Weymouth Sands*.

and run by John and Ellen Gadget. In what remains one of the few instances of sexual fulfillment in the whole of the Powys' canon, ferryman Adam (Jobber) Skald (a native of Portland) and the orphan Perdita Wane consummate their love under the roof of the inn.

In Thomas Hardy's novel *The Well-Beloved*, the angle formed by the junction of Chesil Beach with the island of Portland becomes Deadman's Bay, a reminder of the countless souls lost in this most exposed and treacherous place.

This pleasantly refurbished, beamed and bare boarded eighteenth-century pub has great

The view from the bar and the dining rooms is straight out to sea

views from the three-room bar. The interior is decorated with maritime memorabilia including a detailed map pointing out the location of scores of ships wrecked along the Chesil Beach. In ferocious storms, stones from the beach have been thrown higher than the roof of the pub and come crashing down the chimney.

The ruins of Corfe Castle visited by Ethelberta riding on a donkey!

Castle Inn

Thomas Hardy (1840 - 1928)

Most people do not associate Thomas Hardy with comedy but the author described his novel *The Hand of Ethelberta* as 'A Comedy in Chapters'. Unusually for Hardy, most of the action takes place in London. However, the opening chapters and the exciting conclusion are set here in Dorset. There is a lot of dashing about between the small towns within the Isle of Purbeck. Wareham

appears as Anglebury, Swanage as Knollsea and Corfe Castle becomes Corvesgate Castle (featuring the Castle and The Castle Inn).

The attractive, stone built Castle Inn at Corfe Castle features in Thomas Hardy's novel *The Hand of Ethelberta*, where Corfe becomes Corvesgate.

The young widow Ethelberta, the social climbing heroine, successfully hides the fact that she is one of ten children of a butler. She is determined to win a rich second husband in order to provide for her family and sees an opportunity in Lord Mountclere. The old Lord is entranced by her but will he welcome a butler as a father-in-law?

Mountclere has a house near Swanage but, at the time the novel is set, the railway has not yet reached this far. Consequently a lot of the action takes place along the Anglebury turnpike and there is much involvement with coaches, broughams, chaises and a (horse-drawn) dog-cart. On one occasion Ethelberta's sister Picotee has to wait here in the parlour of The Castle Inn for a rendezvous with her brother Sol and Christopher Julien, Ethelberta's young admirer.

This welcoming little two-room pub has heavy black beams, exposed stone walls, flagstones and open fire. Outside there is a back terrace and a big sunny garden. It is reasonable to believe that Hardy visited the pub and little will has changed since that time.

The little parlour in The Castle Inn where Picotee waited for her brother Sol is now a cosy dining room.

The Cranborne Inn in the heart of the little town was formerly known as Fleur de Lys.

CRANBORNE
Fleur de Lys

Thomas Hardy (1840 - 1928)   Rupert Brooke (1887 - 1915)

In *Tess of the d'Urbervilles*, Cranborne is Thomas Hardy's Chaseborough – the little town set on the edge of the Cranborne Chase where, for centuries, Royalty have had the 'Rights of Chase' and have imposed severe penalties for poaching. With its background of feudal repression, this was the perfect environment for Hardy to use for Alec d'Urberville's rape of his 'pure woman – Tess'.

The original seventeenth-century village bar.

On a Saturday night, Tess's friends from Tantridge 'Pentridge' used to walk to Cranborne and there let their hair down to atone for the monotony of the working week. Sometimes young Tess would join them, but on one fateful Saturday she arrived on her own later than the others. Finding no merry-making at the seventeenth-century Fleur de Lys inn, she was directed to 'a private little jig at a house of a hay-trusser'. Some of the girls had become shy of dancing at the inn:

> *The maids don't think it respectable to dance at 'Flower-de-Luce',*
> *they don't like to let everybody see which be their fancy-men.*

23

As the evening wore on Alec d'Urberville spotted Tess and offered to hire a trap from the pub to drive her home.

The Cranborne Inn was formerly known as the Fleur de Lys. The simply furnished seventeenth-century beamed public bar is so little altered that one could fancy the Tantridge folk had left it the previous evening. One night, before the outbreak of the First World War, the poet Rupert Brooke and his friend Dudley Ward arrived very late into Cranborne. They couldn't find the inn which they had picked out from their guide-book and instead lodged here. Brooke wrote about the experience in a witty poem. The following couple of verses have been sign written on the wall of the bar.

'Mikey' the pub guard dog on his usual seat by the fire.

> *In Cranborne town two inns there are,*
> *And one the Fleur-de-Lys is hight,*
> *And one, the inn Victoria,*
> *Where, for it was alone in sight,*
> *We turned in tired and tearful plight*
> *Seeking for warmth, and company,*
> *And food, and beds so soft and white-*
> *These things are at the Fleur-de-Lys.*
>
> *Where is the ointment for the scar ?*
> *Slippers ? and table deftly dight?*
> *Sofas? tobacco? soap? and ah!*
> *Hot water for a weary wight?*
> *Where is the food, in toil's despite?*
> *The golden eggs? the toast? the tea?*
> *The maid so pretty and polite ?*
> *These things are at the Fleur-de-Lys.*

The King's Arms stands prominently on the right hand side of the Higher East Street incline.

DORCHESTER

King's Arms

Thomas Hardy (1840 - 1928) T. F. Powys (1875 - 1953)

Colin Dexter (1930 -)

Dorset's County Town is the setting for Thomas Hardy's story of Henchard, *The Mayor of Casterbridge*. The author lived at nearby Max Gate, the house he built for himself which is now in the care of The National Trust. He regularly dined in the King's Arms. The ancient inn stands prominently on the right hand side of the Higher East Street incline and above its pillared portico are the distinctive bow windows through which Susan Henchard sees her husband presiding over a dinner surrounded by his Councillors – but drinking only water.

Thomas Hardy's statue, on the roundabout at the top of High West Street and The Grove, commemorates Dorchester's most famous son and one of the great writers of English literature and poetry.

The King's Arms banqueting room where Henchard presided over a dinner surrounded by his councillors.

Henchard sold his wife in a fit of drunken depression at Weydon-Priors country fair eighteen-years previously and the shame led him to a solemn oath to 'avoid all strong liquors for the space of twenty-one years'. Later in the novel Henchard's bankruptcy hearing takes place in the King's Arms. Hardy also mentions the inn in *Under the Greenwood Tree, The Trumpet Major* – and in *Far from the Madding Crowd*, Farmer Boldwood carries Bathsheba inside to recover after she fainted on hearing the news that Troy was thought to be drowned.

T. F Powys calls the pub the Rod and Lion Hotel at Maidenbridge and features it in the opening chapters of *Mr Weston's Good Wine*. In Colin Dexter's *The Way Through the Woods*, Chief Inspector Morse takes a holiday from sleuthing and stays here. Hardy was the detective's second favourite novelist after Dickens, and *The Mayor of Casterbridge* his second favourite novel after *Bleak House*.

Hardy's study has been reconstructed in Dorset County museum Dorchester, just up from the King's Arms.

The sixteenth-century Acorn Inn in Evershot appears as the Sow & Acorn at Evershead, in two of Thomas Hardy's powerful stories: *Interlopers at the Knap* and *The First Countess of Wessex*.

EVERSHOT

Acorn Inn

Thomas Hardy (1840 - 1928)

Set among the rolling hills of West Dorset, in an area of outstanding beauty, the village of Evershot, is Thomas Hardy's Evershead which features in *Tess of the d'Urbervilles*. Tess passes through here on her journey to meet the parents of Angel Clare:

> ...the small town or village of Evershead, being now about half-way over the distance. She made a halt here, and break-fasted a second time, heartily enough – not at the Sow and Acorn, for she avoided inns, but at a cottage by the church.

The church stands towards the top of the long main street and

27

The village bar where in Hardy's *The First Countess of Wessex*, Tupcombe, sat quietly by the fire in the hope of hearing news of Betty.

is unusually dedicated to St Basil, a saint well known to Eastern Orthodox Christianity but almost unheard of in England. One of Jane Austen's favorite poets, George Crabbe (1754-1832), was rector here from 1783-7.

Immediately above the church is Tess' Cottage where she breakfasted and just below the church is the sixteenth-century Acorn Inn which – although Tess avoided – does feature as The Sow & Acorn in two of Hardy's other powerful stories: In *Interlopers at the Knap*, Philip Hall collected Sally's dress that had been left here by the carrier. And in *The First Countess of Wessex*, Squire Dornell's man Tupcombe, sat quietly by the fire in the hope of hearing news of Betty.

The small inn has been very little altered outside, but completely redesigned within. It is built of an attractive mix of stone and brick with a slate roof, fronting directly on to the main street. Pillars support a porch which straddles the pavement and the bay lookout window above is a reminder of the pub's origin as a coaching inn when it was known as The Kings Arms, and brewed its own ales with water drawn from the source of the River Frome.

The main part of the interior has been opened up with a light freshness into a large L-shaped room, formed from three smaller rooms including the inn's original breakfast room. The nine ensuite bedrooms are individually decorated and have their own style and character, each taking a name from one of the characters in *Tess of the d'Urbervilles*. Out towards the back is the 'village bar' with flagstone floor and open fire which still provides some of the atmosphere conveyed by Hardy.

Tess of the d'Urbervilles break-fasted in this cottage on the other side of St Basil's church, just up from The Acorn.

Moonfleet Manor Hotel stands on the edge of the Fleet Water.

Moonfleet Manor

John Meade Falkner (1858 - 1932)

John Meade Falkner was brought up in Dorchester and Weymouth when the tradition of smuggling was still fresh in the minds of the fishing community. He used Fleet, its legends and setting for *Moonfleet*, one of the best adventure stories of the illicit free-trade ever written. Fleet is a unique place with an irregular seawater lagoon separating most of Chesil Beach from the mainland. Here you will find the essential landmarks of the story and a pervading atmosphere of that bygone time.

Central to both story and location is Moonfleet *(Mohune-Fleet)* Manor Hotel which stands on the edge of the Fleet Water at the end of the minor road. The mansion was formerly called Fleet House, built by Maximillion Mohune in 1603, and extended and re-modelled in 1806. Much of it was rebuilt in 1889 – the year following Meade Falkner's story, but there are some remnants of the original Jacobean manor and the Georgian portico remains intact. A foot-path leads from here to a group of cottages at Butter Street.

One of the cottages has been identified as the most likely contender for Elzevir Blocks the Why Not inn which plays such a prominent part in the story. One of the most memorable heart-stopping episodes takes place in the Mohune vault beneath the old church where

The hotel is extravagantly furnished throughout with antique items.

The chancel is all that remains of the old church which was inundated in the great storm of 1824, when the nave was wrecked.

the free-traders hide their contraband and spread rumours of Blackbeard's Ghost haunting the place to keep away the inquisitive.

Though imposing, this family friendly hotel is warm and welcoming and there is no stuffy dress code. There is a spacious bar/restaurant with a timber decking terrace overlooking the countryside and the Fleet Water. Many of the rooms are named after characters in the story including Master Ratsey, Trenchard and Mohune.

This cottage in Butter Street is thought to have been Elzevir Blocks the Why Not inn.

The Horton Inn at Horton on the edge of the Cranborne Chase is Thomas Hardy's Lorton Inn.

HORTON

The Horton Inn

Thomas Hardy (1840 - 1928)

The Horton Inn is located on the edge of Cranborne Chase, eight miles east of Blandford Forum on the B3078 within easy reach of the New Forest. This striking eigh-teenth-century hostelry stands in a commanding open position at Horton Cross where the original turnpike road connecting Poole and Salisbury is intersected by the minor country road from Woodley Down to Ringwood.

There is a welcoming log fire in the dining room.

In his collection of short stories *A Group of Noble Dames*, Hardy had the Horton Inn in mind as the rendezvous for his eloping heroine *Dame the Second – Barbara of the House of Grebe* as told in the old Surgeon's macabre tale. He called it Lornton Inn, and described it as 'the rendezvous of many a daring poacher for operations in the adjoining forest'.

The inn features again later when Barbara goes 'as far as Lornton Inn' to meet her husband Willows who is returning from Southampton. She had to wait and:

There was not much accommodation for a lady at this wayside tavern but, as it was a fine evening in early summer, she did not mind walking about outside. As she waited Barbara became: ... conscious that more eyes were watching her from the inn windows than met her own gaze.

New Forest ales from Ringwood Brewery.

The Horton Inn was at one time a noted posting-house where the London to Exeter stage coaches changed horses. Since then the building has doubled in size by the addition of a wing at right angles to the eighteenth-century original.

The dining room walls are decorated with early photographs of the inn.

LYME REGIS
Bay Hotel
Colin Dexter (1930 -)

To find Chief Inspector Morse miles away from his beloved City of Dreaming Spires; staying on his own in a (guest house type) provincial sea-side hotel that doesn't even serve cask conditioned bitter is rather strange. The Bay Hotel in Lyme is comfortable but bears no comparison with the swish Randolph Hotel – Morse's preferred Oxford haunt.

In the very amusing opening chapter of Colin Dexter's *The Way Through the Woods* we find the detective in a rare mood, contemplating a holiday in the form of a literary tour of Dorset and Somerset and reading the following advertisement in the *Observer*:

Lyme Bay Hotel (seen here from The Cobb) was featured by Colin Dexter in the Inspector Morse detective story *The Way Through the Woods*.

> *Surely one of the finest settings of any hotel in the West Country! We are the only hotel on the Marine Parade and we enjoy panoramic views from Portland Bill to the east, to the historic Cobb Harbour to the west. The hotel provides a high standard of comfort and cuisine, and a friendly relaxed atmosphere. There are level walks to shops and harbour, and traffic-free access to the beach, which is immediately in front of the hotel.*

When Colin Dexter (and his alter ego Morse) stayed here they occupied the room right at the top with magnificent views across the bay. In a press article in 2010 Dexter said:

My favourite place on Earth has to be Lyme Regis. By the time I was 16 I'd read all but one of Hardy's novels – he wrote 17 in all: I'm leaving the last one for my dotage. I was fascinated by Hardy and Wessex, and Lyme Regis, of course, is in the heart of what they call 'Hardy Country'. I fell in love with the Dorset seaside town the first time I visited it many years ago and decided to incorporate it in a novel some day.

When Colin Dexter and his wife stayed here they occupied the room right at the top with the curved roof gable.

I eventually worked the town into a Morse novel, The Way Through the Woods. *I remember telling my publisher at the time to turn to that section because I thought it was the best bit in the book, and the dear girl, who I admired enormously, said she agreed with me but then suggested I leave it out 'and got on with the story'. That rather saddened me – but I didn't take any notice.*

Royal Lion

John Fowles (1926 - 2005)   Jane Austen (1775 - 1817)

Built as a coaching inn in 1601, The Lion as it was known in Jane Austen's time stood in a yard behind the houses that front Broad Street today. In the middle of the nineteenth-century the inn was extended forward by incorporating Broad Street houses into the whole. The Royal prefix appeared after the Prince of Wales (later Edward VII) stayed here in 1856.

The inn appears as the White Lion in John Fowles's brilliant novel *The French Lieutenant's Woman*. Fowles evokes in perfect detail the Victorian world of repressed sexuality and cruel hypocrisy. In the story, Charles Smithson's apartment in the inn incorporates the angular bay window with its famous views up and down Broad Street. Described by Jane Austen as: 'the principal street almost hurrying to the water.'

In Jane Austen's novel *Persuasion*, the whole party gathered at the bay window of their inn to watch as Mr Elliot left Lyme in his curricle.

The Royal Lion Hotel appears as the White Lion in John Fowles's brilliant novel *The French Lieutenant's Woman*.

The inn and the surrounding area were used as the setting for *The French Lieutenant's Woman*, both in the novel and in the film, which was shot on location, starring Jeremy Irons as Smithson and Meryl Streep as the ostracized Sarah Woodruff. Jane Austen stayed in Lyme with her family in the summer of 1804 and used her impressions of the beautiful little seaside town as background for her novel *Persuasion*.

> *...a very strange stranger it must be, who does not see the charms in the immediate environs of Lyme, to make him wish to know it better.*

Although Jane is now believed to have stayed with her family in a cottage on the opposite side of Broad Street, she depicted an inn room in *Persuasion* with the bay window where the Musgroves watched Mr Elliot's curricle leaving Lyme.

The comfortable lounge of the Royal Lion Hotel.

To the left of the entrance in this friendly, family run hotel, there is a cosy beamed lounge bar. And upstairs, just across the landing from the spacious and comfortable dining room is the small Edward VII lounge with its window and famous view.

The steps on the Cobb at Lyme Bay imagined by Jane Austen in *Persuasion* as the scene of Louisa Musgroves's fall.

The Blackmore Vale Inn in the heart of the village of Marnhull appears as Rolliver's in Thomas Hardy's novel *Tess of the d'Urbervilles.*

MARNHULL
Blackmore Vale Inn
Thomas Hardy (1840 - 1928)

Marnhull is Thomas Hardy's Marlott; birthplace of Tess of the d'Urbervilles. The scattered village is located in the northeast corner of the Blackmore Vale; which Hardy described as the 'Vale of Little Dairies, in which the fields are never brown and the springs never dry'. The Blackmore Vale Inn, in the heart of the village, is Rolliver's of the novel.

In the opinion of Tess's father, old John Durbeyfield: 'There's a very pretty brew in the tap at the Pure Drop, though to be sure, not so good as Rolliver's'. And this is what he told Parson Tringham. Today the beer in both pubs is equally good because they are both owned by Dorset brewers Hall & Woodhouse.

It was here at Rolliver's that Parson Tringham told John there was a rich d'Urberville relation living in Trantridge, and so the tragic story that was to become one of the finest novels of the English language was set in motion.

The exterior of the pub belies its 400 year existence. Built originally as farm cottages it later became an old bake-house and brew-house. Today everything about the Blackmore Vale Inn is as welcoming as you could wish. Inside there are two very atmospheric bars having heavily beamed ceilings, bare stone walls and two beautiful open inglenook fireplaces.

The inn sign is taken from the Victorian painting *The Milkmaid* by Henry John King.

At the time of the story however things were very different and Rolliver's is described as a disreputable and illegal drinking house, where only local people in the know were allowed to drink inside – secretly in an upstairs bedroom. The landlady greeted every unknown arrival with: 'Being a few private friends I've asked in to keep up club-walking at my own expense.' Just in case they might be some gaffer sent by Government.

This is the cottage in Marnhull that Hardy imagined as the d'Urbervilles' family home and Tess' birthplace.

The Crown at Marnhull appears as the Pure Drop Inn, Marlott, in Thomas Hardy's novel *Tess of the d'Urbervilles*.

The Crown

Thomas Hardy (1840 - 1928)

This straggling village of stone and thatch cottages is Thomas Hardy's Marlott, with Rolliver's Inn at one end and The Pure Drop Inn at the other. It is the home of Hardy's Tess of the d'Urberville's and the Crown is The Pure Drop Inn'of the novel.

Standing near St Gregory's church, the exterior complex of extensive stone buildings with acres of thatch roof has changed little since Hardy's day. The

central farmhouse of rough stone is mid seventeenth century with wings added in the eighteenth and nineteenth centuries. Before the A30 was turnpiked, Marnhull was on the main coaching route between Shaftesbury and Sherborne and the

The entrance is through a deep porch where the heavy oak front door opens into the big beamed main bar.

The flagged floor in front of the inglenook-fireplace is marked out for the old form of bar skittles.

The partly uncovered priest hole in the main bar.

huge barn facing the Crown's spacious car park suggests its use for large numbers of carriages, horses and their fodder.

The entrance to the 'Pure Drop' is through a deep porch, where a heavy oak door opens into the big main bar with stone walls and steps down to the flagged floor. Leading off from this area are smaller heavily-beamed irregularly shaped rooms used for dining. The floor in front of the inglenook fireplace is marked out for the old form of bar skittles. A priest hole is partly uncovered in the main bar where it leads through into an old panelled room

Along the roadside frontage, a carriage arch shelters under an exterior stone staircase which leads to the first floor of the extension where courts were held. Today the Crown could be described as the crown jewel in Dorset brewer's Hall & Woodhouse estate. They have recently spent lavishly on refurbishment but have been faithful to the essence of this ancient country inn.

The Hunter's Moon at Middlemarsh appears as The Horse on Hintock Green in Thomas Hardy's poem *A Trampwoman's Tragedy*.

MIDDLEMARSH

Hunter's Moon

Thomas Hardy (1840 - 1928)

This 'blink and you'll miss it' hamlet on the A352, features in two of Thomas Hardy's stories. The quartet of itinerant characters in *A Trampwoman's Tragedy* roam through the New Forest and the Blackmore Vale; climb the Mendips, ford the Yeo river near Yeovil and head on through the Marshwood Fens:

The inn sign with its depiction of a barn owl graphically illustrates the concept of a hunter's moon.

> *From Wynyard's Gap the livelong day,*
> *The livelong day,*
> *We beat afoot the northward way*
> *We had travelled times before.*
> *The sun-blaze burning on our backs,*
> *Our shoulders sticking to our packs,*
> *By fosseway, fields, and turnpike tracks*
> *We skirted sad Sedge-Moor.*

Lone inns we loved, my man and I,
My man and I;
'King's Stag,' 'Windwhistle' high and dry,
'The Horse' on Hintock Green,
The cosy house at Wynyard's Gap,
'The Hut' renowned on Bredy Knap,
And many another wayside tap
Where folk might sit unseen.

Four of the 'lone inns' they visit are still in existence: The inn at Winyard's Gap, the Windwhistle Inn at Cricket St Thomas near Crewkerne, the Green Man at King's Stag and this one; which until recently was known as the White Horse, but in Hardy's story it is The Horse on Hintock Green. The essence of Hardy's novel *The Woodlanders* revolves around this small rural community which he calls the Hintocks centred on Middlemarsh.

The present roadside frontage of the Hunter's Moon, with its three ground floor bay windows is unchanged since Hardy's day when his friend, pioneer photographer Hermann Lea, described it as:

The Winyards Gap Inn is another of the four extant inns known to the Trampwoman and her travelling companions. This area is famous for its stunning scenery and views. From the terraces and bars, on a clear day, you can see the Blackdown, Mendip and Quantock hills as well as Glastonbury. 'The River Parrett Trail' starts just south of the inn and the 'The Monarch's Way' passes right by.

a picturesque building of weatherworn brick; the tiled roof is laid to a pattern and the tiles themselves are moss-grown, the chimneys are massive and elaborated with dentil courses under the copings.

Much extended now, but with great sympathy, the comfortably welcoming beamed interior rambles around in several linked areas. A cosy, soft-lit relaxed intimacy is created with loads of bric-a-brac, open log fires and a great variety of tables, chairs and booths created from settles.

The Brace of Pheasants appears as the Quiet Drop, Netherplash Cantorum in Cecil Day-Lewis's Nicholas Blake story *The Deadly Joker*.
Photo courtesy of Graham Rains

PLUSH
Brace of Pheasants
Cecil Day-Lewis (1904 - 1972)

This picturesque inn is constructed from two sixteenth-century cottages and a forge. It became an inn in the mid 1930s and in the 1950s, pub trade novices Joan and John Elven, took it over. It was soon included in the *Good Food Guide* thanks to Joan's culinary skills and her quiet charm as 'Mine Hostess'. Notable people came to stay including Cecil Day-Lewis who first stayed here with his actress wife Jill Balcon in May 1960.

Day-Lewis became Poet Laureate in 1968 but he was also a successful thriller writer under the non-de-plume of Nicholas Blake. His novel *The Deadly Joker* is dedicated to Joan and Jo and set in Plush with many of the scenes taking place in the pub. In the story the village becomes Netherplash Cantorum, and the inn appears as the Quiet Drop.

The unique pub sign with a brace of pheasants in a glass display case.

The Brace's cosy bar.

The story begins with a cuckoo calling out in the dead of night preventing pub guests, writer John Waterson – and his much younger wife Jenny – from getting to sleep. A number of the characters in the story are drawn from Day-Lewis's own family and friends. Vera Paston, 'A passion-flower among the primroses', is based on an Indian novelist with whom he was involved in 1961/2.

Cecil Day-Lewis' black marble headstone stands next to the Hardy family graves in Stinsford chuchyard.

John Waterson's son Sam has some of the traits of Day-Lewis's own journalist son, Sean. And Sean notes some specific examples of this in his biography of his father; including the fact that a real cuckoo did keep Cecil and Jill awake on their first stay at the Brace.

Plush is a timeless place hidden in a small side-valley of the River Piddle about 8 miles north of Dorchester. The Brace is a picture-postcard perfect pub. Think thatched cottage, open fire, skittle alley and a Tolkien-like interior and you'll be pretty close to the mark. Although Day-Lewis was from Ireland he came to love Dorset. He also acknowledged that the poet who influenced him most was Thomas Hardy and his final wish was fulfilled when he was laid to rest in Stinsford churchyard near the spot where Hardy's heart is buried.

Plush is thought to be Hardy's village of Flintcombe Ash in *Tess of the d'Urbervilles*. The cottage in the background on the left (as seen from the pub) is where Tess sheltered from the rain and warmed herself against the wall.
Photo courtesy of Graham Rains

The Digby Tap in Sherborne is all that remains of the former chief hostelry of the town which featured in Thomas Hardy's novel *The Woodlanders*. In the story the town became Sherton Abbas and the hotel the Earl of Wessex.

SHERBORNE
Digby Tap

Thomas Hardy (1840 - 1928)   John Le Carré (1931 -)

In the *The Woodlanders*, Thomas Hardy tells us that:

> *The chief hotel at Sherton Abbas was the 'Earl of Wessex' – a substantial inn of Ham-hill stone with a yawning back yard into which vehicles were driven by coachmen to stabling of wonderful commodiousness.*

Sherton Abbas is the small, exquisite Abbey town of Sherborne: and its then chief hostelry was the Digby Hotel. One of the most dramatic incidents in the story takes place in the yawning back yard where Giles Winterborne has set up his mobile apple-mill and cider press. From one of the inn windows, Grace Melbury sees Giles for the first time since becoming another man's wife.

The main building of this once prestigious coaching inn is

now used to accommodate students of Sherborne School, with the former stables and out-buildings being converted into luxury apartments. However, there is a tiny part that continues as a thriving pub – and for many, including me, the old Digby Tap room is the perfect pub. However, this is not the place for those seeking sophistication. If you like

down-to-earth old fashioned ale houses, then this splendid example of a basic town local is for you.

Sherborne School and the Digby Tap also have another more modern literary connection. Though it was obviously never pretentious, the old pub was deliberately de-smartened in the

The interior of the Digby Tap has a relaxed friendly atmosphere, plenty of character and attracts a mix of all ages and walks of life.

The film of John Le Carré's thriller *Murder of Quality* starring Denholm Elliot, Glenda Jackson and Joss Ackland, was shot on location in Sherborne and the Digby Tap.

Old brewery advertising signs enhance the simple decor throughout the series of small rooms.

49

early 1990s to suit its use for filming a 1962 John Le Carré thriller *Murder of Quality* starring Denholm Elliot, Glenda Jackson and Joss Ackland and there are framed stills from the movie hanging in the bar. Le Carré is a Dorset man: he was born in Poole and educated here at Sherborne School but the story involves a murder at Eton where he became a school-master.

The interior of the Digby Tap feels as comfortable as a favourite old sweater. Advertising signs from bygone brew-erys enhance the simple decor throughout the series of small rooms with flagstone-floors and traditional seating; plus a warning that you will be fined (proceeds to charity) for using a mobile phone. The relaxed friendly atmosphere has plenty of character and attracts a mix of all ages and walks of life. Just round the corner is the glorious golden stone Abbey but the Digby Tap is sufficiently tucked away for only the more adventurous tourists to find it.

SWANAGE
Ship Inn
Enid Blyton (1897 - 1968)

The Ship Inn Swanage where Enid Blyton brought her daughters in May 1940 for the first of many holidays staying in the town.

Enid Blyton's love affair with Dorset began with her first visit at Easter in 1931 when she was 34 and pregnant with her first child. She would later return to spend many holidays in and around the town of Swanage in South Dorset's 'Isle of Purbeck'. In March 1940 she brought her two daughters, Gillian and Imogen here for a holiday and they shared a room at the Ship Inn which is located in the very centre of the town opposite the square overlooking Swanage Bay.

Over a forty year period, Enid Blyton wrote in excess of 600 books, including *The Famous Five* series which have very apparent Purbeck connections. The *Famous Five* comprise four decidedly upper-class children with a mongrel dog who solve mysteries and get tangled up with smugglers and other criminals. Naturally the children arrive for their holiday on a steam train like those still running on the heritage line from Corfe to Swanage. They want nothing more than to have a great time roaming about the countryside and having picnics, but adventures just keep coming along and getting in the way.

The steam train that brought the Blyton family to the seaside, seen here crossing the viaduct at Corfe Castle, continues to operate today as a heritage railway.

It is not always possible to exactly match Enid's description's with actual places but Kirrin Castle is clearly based on Corfe:

On a low hill rose the ruined castle. It had been built of big white stones. Broken archways, tumbledown towers, ruined walls – that was all there was left of a once beautiful castle, proud and strong. Now the jackdaws nested in it.

Five Go Down to the Sea, first published in 1953, is the twelfth novel in the *Famous Five* series.

And Enid admitted that Whispering Island in *Five Have A Mystery To Solve,* was modelled on Brownsea Island in Poole Harbour.

Enid's pleasure at the prospect of a visit to Swanage never palled. In her *Adventure of the Strange Ruby* she identifies both Swanage and Corfe Castle by their real names: 'We're going somewhere for the hols,' says Faith. 'If only it was Swanage again!'

Swanage is described in the story as:

Enid Blyton's, *The Rubadub Mystery,* involves another group of children who stay at an old-fashioned inn with oak beams.

just the same as ever – a great wide bay of forget-me-not-blue, with hardly a ripple or wave, except just at the edge. Behind rose the glorious hills.

The Rubadub Mystery, involves another group of children who stay at an old-fashioned inn with oak beams. This makes the children feel as if they have 'gone back hundreds of years' to a time of smugglers. There's not much 'Olde Worlde' about the interior of the Ship today. It has the look and feel of a modern town pub and has become an established music venue.

The Old Ship at Upwey features in Thomas Hardy's most light-hearted novel *Under the Greenwood Tree.*

UPWEY
The Old Ship

Thomas Hardy (1840 - 1928)

The Old Ship at Upwey is located on the old Roman road between Weymouth and Dorchester and features in Thomas Hardy's most light-hearted novel *Under the Greenwood Tree.* The two main characters Dick Dewy the carrier (who is a bit wet) and Fancy Day the pretty young school-teacher (who is a bit airy-fairy) rest here for a while at the inn where they eventually get round to making a commitment to each other.

The Old Ship started life in 1647 as 3 cottages – plus a blacksmith's forge at one end and stables at the other. The white painted exterior has not changed since Hardy was here other than the 'mast and cross-trees' sign he describes has gone.

However, there is a Victorian photograph in the pub showing the mast as he, and generations before him, would have known it when this narrow steep hill was the main thoroughfare between the coast and the county town.

Here and there, old timbers, stone flags and open fireplaces complement the cosy interior which is now open-plan; leading through doorways and arches, and up and down steps in an unrestricted way. In Hardy's day the rooms would have had doors for privacy and the separation of social classes. The 'little tea-room' into which Fancy is ushered would no-doubt have been a private parlour.

> *Half an hour afterwards Dick emerged from the inn, and if Fancy's lips had been real cherries probably Dick's would have appeared deeply stained.*

When the newly betrothed young man returned to the inn yard, the jovial publican smited him playfully under the fifth rib, and said in broad Dorset:

> *This will never do, upon my life, Master Dewy! calling for tay and for a feymel passenger, and then going in and sitting down and having some too, and biding such a fine long time!*

Old timbers, stone flags and open fireplaces complement the interior which is now open-plan; leading through doorways and arches, and up and down steps.

Red Lion

Thomas Hardy (1840 - 1928)

In his construction of 'Wessex' as a region, Hardy used a mixture of real and fictional names for landscape features, towns and villages. And so it is that King Alfred's famous Saxon walled town of Wareham becomes 'Anglebury' – the setting for a novel described by Thomas Hardy as 'A Comedy in Chapters'.

In *The Hand of Ethelberta* the social climbing heroine successfully hides the origin of her family background. The young widow is determined to win a rich husband in order to provide for her father and nine siblings. Lord Mountclere is entranced by her but how will he feel when he finds out that Ethelberta is the daughter of a butler? Could a Lord possibly countenance a butler as a father-in-law?

The Red Lion, Wareham, features in Thomas Hardy's novel *The Hand of Ethelberta* where he calls the town Anglebury.

The first act opens and plays out in:

A Street in Anglebury – A Heath near It – Inside the Red Lion Inn: Young Mrs Petherwin (Ethelberta) stepped from the door of an old and well appointed inn in a Wessex town to take a country walk. By her look and carriage she appeared

*to belong to that gentle order of society which has no worldly
sorrow except when its jewellery is stolen…*

The pub sign - a very modern interpretation of an old theme.

Most of the action in the novel takes place in London, but the opening chapters and the nail-biting conclusion are set in Dorset.

*Two years and a half after the marriage of Ethelberta and the
evening adventures which followed it, a man young in years,
though considerably older in mood and expression, walked
up to the Red Lion Inn at Anglebury… His way of entering
the inn and calling for a conveyance was more off-hand than
formerly… He wanted to be taken to Knollsea [Swanage] to
meet the steamer there, and was not coming back by the same
vehicle.*

The original fourteenth-century inn, standing on the same spot known as the Town Cross, was destroyed in the Great Fire of Wareham in 1762 and the present building dates from that time. In the summer of 2011, after many years of neglect, the Red Lion at Wareham was rescued. The careful refurbishment has restored the building to its original Georgian elegance.

The bar is decorated with large displays of famous folk associated with Dorset - but surprisingly nothing about Hardy.

There is a formal restaurant, relaxed snug dining area and comfortable bar decorated with large displays of famous folk associated with Dorset – but surprisingly nothing about

Hardy. In the partly covered courtyard there are illustrations of various types of horse-drawn conveyances – many of which were available for hire from the inn at the time the novel was set.

The Old Rooms Inn on Weymouth quay features in Thomas Hardy's tale, *A Committee-Man of The Terror*, who put up here. The hostelry also features in *The Dynasts*, the author's vast work in blank verse and prose.

WEYMOUTH
Old Rooms Inn
Thomas Hardy (1840 - 1928)

Weymouth is Thomas Hardy's Budmouth, and the Old Rooms Inn – situated at the old harbour quayside in the most historic and least changed part of the town – features in a couple of his stories. The present Old Rooms Inn is a Georgian extension to the seventeenth-century original, which is still there. You need to walk to the water's edge and look back to appreciate the juxtaposition of the now conjoined buildings; separated in time by one-and-a-half centuries. A tablet on the original building explains that the new wing was added in the 1760s to provide for balls and concerts.

This ancient harbour area is the territory of Hardy's tale: *A Committee-Man of The Terror*, who put up at the Old Rooms

Inn. The hostelry also features in *The Dynasts*, the author's vast work in blank verse and prose which occupied him to some degree throughout his life. Here we find the town burghers and boatmen sitting around speculating on the transportation of Nelson's body, which had been preserved in a barrel of spirits following his death at the Battle of Trafalgar.

The assembled pipe-smoking locals concluded that the Admiral had been his men's salvation after death – as he had been in during the fight. The crew of the *Victory* were so broken down in battle, and hardly able to keep afloat, they drank the barrel dry '... 'twas a most defendable thing, and it fairly saved their lives'.

The exterior of the two-storey Old Rooms Inn is classic symmetrical red-brick Georgian. Although the ground floor has had a later shop-front type of conversion providing large windows for much of the length with views across the harbour. In addition there is now a modern conservatory dining room to the front right hand side with a patio area, making the most of the opportunity from the holiday visitor trade.

Weymouth's original seventeenth-century Assembly Rooms now adjoined to the Old Rooms Inn. The notice above the blue door reads: *'This early 17th century house formed Weymouth's first assembly rooms in the 1760s, when a new wing was added for balls and concerts'*.

The Sailor's Return on Weymouth quay features as 'The Sailor's Rest' in Minette Walters unsettling crime novel *The Shape of Snakes*.

WEYMOUTH
The Sailor's Return
Minette Walters (1949 -)

The Sailor's Return on Weymouth quay is the inspiration for Minette Walters' The Sailor's Rest, in her 2000 thriller *The Shape of Snakes*. This basic town tavern is a little removed from the main tourist area of the old harbour. It is located among tall warehouses on the gas-works side of the swing bridge and has the authentic feel of the type of pub a retired London policeman might take on.

The story, written in the first person, concerns a Mrs Ranelagh (known as M) who lives in south-west London and her twenty-year quest to unravel the truth behind the violent death of her black neighbour, 'Mad Annie'. The concept of the story was inspired by the Stephen Lawrence Inquiry, which was set up to investigate the death of a black boy by a group of white youths.

Two decades after the London happenings the action moves to Dorset with scenes set in various locations including Tout Quarry and the Prison on the Isle of Portland and the Sailor's Return – Weymouth's deep sea angler's pub where some evenings you may see the charter boats unloading and weighing the day's catch.

In chapter twenty of the novel Mrs Ranelagh walks along Weymouth harbour quay and enters the pub. She is here to confront the landlord; the former corrupt and racist police sergeant Drury:

The bar in this basic unfussy town pub is decorated with a nautical theme.

Drury was watching me when I came through the door of the Sailor's Rest at half-past ten that evening. Being a Friday night in summer, the pub was crowded with holiday makers and yachtsmen from the boats in the marina, and I felt a small satisfaction when I saw the flicker of apprehension in his eyes as I approached. He came out from behind the bar before I could reach it. 'We'll go through to the back,' he said curtly, jerking his head toward a door in the corner. 'I'm damned if I'll have this conversation in public.' 'Why not?' I asked. 'Are you afraid of witnesses?'

Minette Walters was born in Dorset and lives and works today in a lovely manor house near Dorchester. The Sailor's Return is an unfussy locals' pub. The bar is decorated with a nautical theme and the largest room is given over to a pool table, juke box and large screen TV.

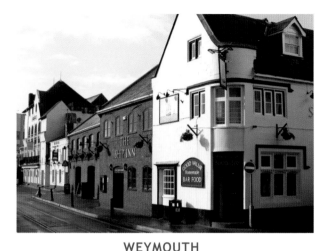

The Ship Inn on Weymouth's Custom House Quay features as 'The Weeping Woman' in J. C. Powys's novel 'Weymouth Sands'.

WEYMOUTH

Ship Inn

John Cowper Powys (1872 - 1963)

The island of Portland and Weymouth's network of streets, terraces, esplanade and harbour provide the setting for J. C. Powys's novel *Weymouth Sands*. The main character, ferry man and carrier, Adam (Jobber) Skald, drinks in The Weeping Woman, run by Miss Guppy. As we follow his hurried walk through the town to his preferred pub, clues eventually lead us down Maiden Street to the present day Ship Inn on Custom House Quay:

> *The perturbed man now crossed the road and leaving the old King's statue before him plunged into the town... he scarce had time to beat down the image of Perdita before he came along the dark warehouses and narrow alleyways and reached the Tap Entrance of the Weeping Woman.*

Later we find Jobber taking Perdita into his old haunt and we learn through her that:

The Weeping Woman was so close to the harbour's edge that at one moment she thought she could hear the lapping of the water.

Weymouth harbour at sunset with the Ship Inn on the left.

One of the most remarkable features of the author's career is – with the exception of *Maiden Castle* – all his great Wessex novels were penned in America. *Weymouth Sands* was written from memories of childhood holidays and local guide books sent to him by his brother.

A modern extension – four times the size of the original stone-built Elizabethan Ship Inn – now extends along the front of the quay. Although the modern interior is spacious and open plan it has been divided up into smaller friendly drinking and dining areas. Wooden floors, sympathetic colours and plenty of nautical brick-a-brac combine to make it feel welcoming.

Proof of antiquity can be found by walking a little way up Maiden Street past the back door of the pub – the original Tap Room entrance used by Jobber Skald. Here, lodged high in the gable end stonework of the adjoined building, is a cannon ball from a shot fired in the Civil War in 1645.

A cannon ball from a shot fired in the Civil War in 1645 is lodged high in the gable end stonework near the original Tap Room entrance used by Jobber Skald.

EARLY 17TH CENTURY BUILDINGS
(SHIP INN TO DUKE OF CORNWALL)

THE GABLE END SHOWS
PROBABLE CANNON SHOT DAMAGE
FROM THE CIVIL WAR, 1645

ish of Oare, in the county of Somerset, yeoman and churchwarden, hav
n and had a share in some doings of this neighborhood, which I will tr
et down in order, God sparing my life and memory. And they who ligh
on this book should bear in mind not only that I write for the clearin
ur parish from ill fame and calumny, but also a thing which will, I trov
bear too often in it, to wit—that I am nothing more than a plain unlet
ed man, not read in foreign languages, as a gentleman might be, nc
ed with long words (even in mine own tongue), save what I may hav
n from the Bible or Master William Shakespeare, whom, in the face c
mon opinion, I do value highly. In short, I am an ignoramus, but prett
l for a yeoman.

Somerset

My father being of good substance, at least as we reckon in Exmoor, an
red in his own right, from many generations, of one, and that the be
l largest, of the three farms into which our parish is divided (or rathe
cultured part thereof), he John Ridd, the elder, churchwarden, an
rseer, being a great admirer of learning, and well able to write his nam
t me his only son to be schooled at Tiverton, in the county of Devor
the chief boast of that ancient town (next to its woollen staple) is
rthy grammar-school, the largest in the west of England, founded an
ndsomely endowed in the year 1604 by Master Peter Blundell, of tha
e place, clothier.

Here, by the time I was twelve years old, I had risen into the uppe
ool, and could make bold with Eutropius and Caesar—by aid of a
glish version—and as much as six lines of Ovid. Some even said that
ght, before manhood, rise almost to the third form, being of a perseve
nature; albeit, by full consent of all (except my mother), thick-heade
t that would have been, as I now perceive, an ambition beyond a farmer
; for there is but one form above it, and that made of masterful scholar
itled rightly 'monitors'. So it came to pass, by the grace of God, that
called away from learning, whilst sitting at the desk of the junior fir
he upper school, and beginning the Greek verb.

My eldest grandson makes bold to say that I never could have learned
pages further on, being all he himself could manage, with plenty

The 500 year old Globe, features in Peter Benson's novel *Two Cows and a Vanful of Smoke.* Photo courtesy of John Short

APPLEY
The Globe
Peter Benson (1956 -)

This wonderful 500 year old pub features in Peter Benson's novel *Two Cows and a Vanful of Smoke.*

> *The Globe at Appley was a pub, but it was more like a house. You walked in the front door and into a corridor, and a fat woman with purple legs served the drinks from a hatch in the corridor. There was a bench you could sit on and a room with a dart board. She was a strict woman, and would have you out of there if you cursed God or said something about the Queen she didn't agree with, so I bought my beer and went to sit in the porch.*

Benson's story is set in a largely undiscovered part of Somerset among the hills, fields, farms, woods and narrow high-hedged lanes to the west of Wellington. This is where young

Elliot, the main character lives and where his dubious former school-friend Spike continually leads him into trouble. Written in Benson's distinctive style with echoes of Laurie Lee and J.D. Salinger, this is a tale of misplaced loyalty, which unexpectedly develops into an unconventional but believable thriller.

The small linked drinking/dining rooms are full of quirky interest.

The Globe started life as two cottages and the corridor, with its polished red quarry tile floor and whitewashed arched ceiling and walls, was the access between them. The hatch through which the drinks are dispensed was once the front room window of the right hand cottage. There are a number

of small linked drinking/dining rooms which are full of quirky interest. The strict former landlady was Mrs Endicott who died in the 1980s. She had been resident for thirty years and before her the pub was in the same family for eighty years.

The 'corridor' bar was once the front room of the right-hand cottage

Another nice pub: The Inn at Staple Cross, Hockworthy, also features in the story where country lore and old superstitions have not been forgotten.

ASHCOTT
The Pipers Inn

Parson James Woodforde (1740 – 1803)

William Wordsworth (1770 – 1850)

In the 1760s when William Wordsworth was just a boy, the gentle and generous Parson Samuel Woodforde paid regular visits to The Pipers Inn. This was when he was curate at Thurloxton and was travelling backwards and forwards between there and his home at Ansford. He recorded seven of these occasions in his now famous *The Diary of a Country Parson*, providing details of his dinner, breakfast, corn for his horse, the landlord's name and the amount he tipped the ostler and the maid who waited on him. On 10 October 1763 he tells us that:

> *I had half a pint of mountain and two Eggs at Piper's Inn about one o'clock and that served for a Dinner. Piper's Inn*

The Pipers Inn, where Wordsworth breakfasted, comprises two adjoined buildings of different periods and architectural styles.

is kept by one Beadon. For my Wine & Eggs and Horse pd.
0 – 0 – 9 Gave to Hostler there 0 – 0 – 2.

And on 12 November of the same year he says he met up here at The Piper's Inn with Young Captain Rooke:

Where we both dined… For eating at the Piper's Inn I paid
0 – 3 – 0 Gave the Waiting Maid there 0 – 0 – 6 Gave the
Hostler there 0 – 0 – 3.

As you can see from the photograph, The Pipers Inn now comprises two buildings of contrasting architectural styles. A former inn on this site called The Castle appears to have been rebuilt, possibly in the late seventeenth century. The Pipers Inn is recorded in 1723 and there are a number of romantic and prosaic reasons given for the name. Whatever the truth, an inn has stood on this site for over 400 years. About 200 years ago an imposing house was added to the side of the existing building to form the present day frontage. No

The soft light in the lounge is provided by the floor to ceiling Georgian windows.

attempt was made to match the architectural styling or roof lines of the original building and hence we have the rather odd external appearance of the pub today.

In 1841, two years before he succeeded Robert Southey as Poet Laureate, Wordsworth returned to Somerset on a nostalgic trip to visit his youthful haunts. He and his wife Mary stayed at a friend's house in Bath and on 29 April, the *Bath Chronicle* briefly announced his presence in the city:

THE FAMOUS GROUSE
FAMOUS PUBS

THE PIPERS INN

A LANDMARK COACHING INN IN THE 1700S, THE PIPERS INN WAS NOTED IN THE FAMOUS 'WOODFORDE DIARIES', ITS AUTHOR REVEREND JAMES WOODFORDE ENJOYED THE EXPERIENCE SO MUCH THAT HE TIPPED THE MAID 3 PENNIES.

2011

"FAMOUS FOR A REASON"

Visits by Parson Woodforde and William Wordsworth are both celebrated with 'Famous Grouse' plaques.

> *The distinguished poet Wordsworth is at present residing in Bath, where we understand he will remain until the middle of June.*

Towards the end of his visit he attended the wedding of his only daughter, Dora, to Mr Edward Quillinan at St James's church. One day the wedding party drove out to Ashcott to have breakfast at The Pipers Inn and afterwards they all went to Alfoxden where the poet sought reminiscences of his past.

Today The Pipers stands bold and defiant against the incessant traffic speeding past along the A39. There is a large welcoming beamed lounge with wood burning stove and comfortable leather armchairs. And this former coaching inn enjoys a good reputation for a wide choice of reasonably priced food – although they no longer serve breakfasts!

Magnolia Grandiflora
festooning the façade
identifies the Royal
Crescent Hotel.

BATH

Royal Crescent Hotel

Colin Dexter (1930 -)

In Colin Dexter's *Death is Now My Neighbour*, murder first strikes in an old Oxfordshire village. Investigations begin to unearth links with the academic world and the hunt for clues takes Morse and Lewis into the hot-house atmosphere of college elections and eventually down to the West Country city of Bath.

Morse stood for some while on the huge slabs that form the wide pavement stretching along the whole extent of the great 500-foot curve of the cinnamon-coloured stone, with its iden-

tical facades of double Ionic columns, which comprise Bath's Royal Crescent. It seemed to him a breathtaking architectural masterpiece, with the four-star hotel at its centre: Number 16.

In this story Morse's over-fondness for real ale and single malt whiskies finally catches up with him and he is diagnosed with diabetes. The Royal Crescent Hotel first features when a murder suspect uses a stay here as an alibi. Then, after the case is successfully concluded, Morse returns for a

A luxury dining experience awaits.

few days' break from Oxford accompanied by the nursing sister who tended him in hospital. The hotel's opulent atmosphere and his new affair prove such a heady and weakening mix that, in a rare display of gratitude, Morse sends Lewis an aerial view picture postcard of the city with a touching message signed: 'Yours aye, Endeavour (Morse)'; thereby

The garden Dower House restaurant and accommodation annex.

finally revealing the closely guarded secret of his Christian name.

As ever, Colin Dexter's description is razor sharp, which you can verify if you are willing and able to pay for the luxury bed & breakfast experience on offer.

The hotel is a Grade I listed building of the greatest historical and architectural importance. Completed by 1775, it was completely refurbished in 1998 and the work undertaken has restored many of the classical Georgian features with all the additional modern comforts. Among the celebrities staying here on the day I called was Kriss Akabusi, Midge Ure, Lenny Henry and Felicity Kendal.

The welcoming grand entrance and staircase.

The Sam Wellers unusual and attractive pub sign.

BATH

Sam Wellers

Charles Dickens (1812 – 1870)

Sam Wellers at 13-14
Upper Borough Walls.

On arrival at Bath, Mr Pickwick and his friends: '…respectfully retired to their private sitting rooms at the White Hart Hotel, opposite the great Pump Room'.

This magnificent inn (now gone) was owned in Dickens' time by one Moses Pickwick who also ran a coaching business from here. In the story, Sam Weller receives an invitation from his fellow footmen to a

The bright and welcoming dining room. The walls are decorated with Dickensian prints and cartoons.

social evening described as a 'leg o' mutton swarry' and:

> *Sam at once beetook himself into the presence of Mr Pick-*
> *wick, and requested leave of absence for that evening, which*
> *was readily granted. With this permission, and the street-*
> *door key, Sam issued fourth a little before the appointed time,*
> *and strolled leisurely towards Queen Square, which he had*
> *no sooner gained than he had the satisfaction of beholding*
> *Mr John Smaulker.*

The companions walked together from Queen Square towards High Street, turning down a side street along the way. Clues lead to this tavern which was either: 'the small greengrocer's shop' in whose parlour the Bath footmen held their social evenings; or the public-house from which, we are told, drinks includ- ing 'cold srub* and water, gin and sweet water and a large bowl of punch' were fetched for that dignified occasion.

Either way, this is an interesting and atmospheric city centre pub. It was obviously known (and most likely frequented by Dickens) as it stands obliquely across a narrow road junction from the prominent city land- mark of the Royal National Hospital for Rheumatic Diseases established in 1739.

This friendly, centrally-situated city pub receives consistently good reviews for its real ale and unpreten- tious wholesome food.

*Srub (or shrub), if you are wondering, is a drink made from orange or lemon juice, sugar, and rum or brandy.

This attractive triple-gabled tavern at 42 Broad Street was host to Charles Dickens in 1835.

Saracen's Head

Charles Dickens (1812 – 1870)

The Saracen's Head is proud of its Dickens associations; the actual chair he sat in, the actual jug he drank from, and the actual room he slept in are each shown with much ado to visitors; whilst several anecdotes associated with the novelist's visit on the occasion are re-told with perfect assurance of their truth.

So B.W.Matz tells us in *The Inns and Taverns of Pickwick*, writing in 1921 with his pen in his hand and his tongue in his cheek. Dickens did stay here in 1835 during his journalistic days when following Lord John Russell through the country and reporting his speeches. But at that time Dickens was an unknown, and no one other than the author himself, would remember his stay at the Saracen's Head. Such was Dickens' eventual fame, the proprietors were more than happy to promote the connection, fifty years after the author's death. Although there is no reference to Dickens in the pub today.

As a humble (yet observant) reporter Dickens was obliged to stay in this back street inn whilst Lord John Russell no doubt sojourned at the White Hart – Bath's most prestigious

The Saracens Head colourful sign.

establishment owned by a Mr Moses Pickwick (who also ran a stage coach business). Dickens's later used his memories of Bath to wonderful effect in *Pickwick Papers.*

The Saracen's Head stands at 42 Broad Street, and has a rear entrance opening onto Walcot Street. This attractive triple-gabled tavern built in 1713, is one of Bath's earliest buildings

The entrance from the stable yard which Dickens would have used is now a feature inside the dining room.

The ceiling in the main bar is one of the original remaining period features.

and the city's oldest pub. It is easy to lose direction among the various odd-shaped 'Dickensian' rooms and bars. However, the sense of antiquity is dulled by the fact that the original fabric is hidden behind a modern 'Olde Worlde' façade.

The rear entrance opens onto Walcot Street.

BRISTOL

Llandoger Trow

Daniel Defoe (1660 - 1731)   M. R. Hall (1967 -)

Famous privateer Captain Woodes Rogers, lived just round the corner from the Llandoger Trow. Weighing anchor off the island of Juan Fernandez on 2 February 1709, he happened on the marooned sailor Alexander Selkirk and later returned with him to Bristol. When Daniel Defoe came to Bristol in 1713 (to escape his creditors) the story of Selkirk's adventure was already

well known and he was keen to meet the intrepid survivor. Defoe's earliest biographer says the couple met at Mrs Damaris Davies' house in St James Square but persistent local tradition has it that they met here in the Llandoger Trow.

Originally three merchant's houses, the 'Llandoger Trow' dates back to the mid seventeenth-century.

My own feeling is that they would have met a number of times and, if so, why not have a chat over a tot of grog in this atmospheric inn? Anyway, Defoe embellished the story adding many incidents from his own imagining and in 1719 published *The Life and strange surprising adventures of Robinson Crusoe*.

The name Llandoger Trow is unique among inns and has a historical significance. A trow was a flat-bottomed boat which traded from the Welsh Back, harbour area of Bristol up the Wye Valley on a regular service.

The ornately carved over-mantle above the fireplace in the bar.

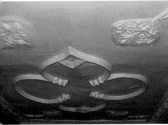

Impressive plaster ceilings abound.

For over ten years Matthew Hall has been a screen writer and producer, and has written over forty hours of prime time drama for BBC1 and ITV. His debut novel, *The Coroner*, introducing the character of Jenny Cooper, was nominated for the Crime Writer's Association Gold Dagger in the best novel category. *The Mother*, to be published in January 2014, is the sixth novel in the series and features the Llandoger Trow. Matthew says:

This pub is one of my favourites as I live near the village of Llandogo the other side of the Severn and up the Wye ten miles. My property includes some woodland on a hillside, which until early twentieth century was a quarry from which millstones were cut by hand. The stones were rolled a mile down the hill to the river Wye, where the Llandogo Trow would pick them up and ferry them over to Bristol to be unloaded at the docks.

Many of the original buildings in King Street were erected between 1650 and 1665 as merchants' houses. Three of these, which comprise the present-day inn, survived the 1940 blitz. No. 5 has been the Llandoger Trow for at least two centuries

and restoration in the 1960s uncovered seven fireplaces, some fine original Georgian pine panelling, Delft tiles and some beautiful plaster-work. The original seventeenth-century oak stairs connecting all the floors now leads up to the restaurants.

Each of the numerous dining areas that comprise the first-floor restaurant have individual period fire places.

The tavern entrance in the court leading to the old St Nicholas flower market.

Rummer Tavern

Samuel Taylor Coleridge (1772 - 1834)

Robert Southey (1774 - 1843)

William Wordsworth (1770 - 1850)

William Wordsworth, recalled of his *Lines written a few miles above Tintern Abbe:* 'I began it upon leaving Tintern and concluded it just as I was entering Bristol'. It was finished in Joseph Cottle's parlour whose bookshop was round the corner from the Rummer. And the poem was published as part of *The Lyrical Ballads,* by Cottle who was so central to the support of Wordsworth, Coleridge and Southey during their West Country sojourn.

Southey lived across the road from the tavern where he used to meet up with Wordsworth and Coleridge.

Southey was born in Bristol in a house which stood diagonally across the road from the Rummer (there is a plaque on

This dark narrow passageway, which now leads to the toilets, was once part of the original bar. The ancient fireplace, where the poets sat around discussing their Pantisocracy scheme, is now protected behind a perspex screen.

the present-day building). At Oxford in 1794 he met Coleridge who filled his head with dreams of an American utopian community where selfishness was to be extinguished, and the virtues were to reign supreme. Coleridge and Southey soon met again at Bristol, and with Robert Lovell they developed their 'Pantisocracy' idea – often discussing emigration plans over drinks at the Rummer.

Finance was the problem and Coleridge devised the fund-raising idea of publishing a magazine to be called *The Watchman*. He convened his friends to a meeting at the Rummer, to determine the size, price, and frequency 'with all other preliminaries, essential to the launching this first-rate vessel on the mighty deep'. Unfortunately, after only ten issues the vessel sunk, and the long-suffering Cottle, once again stepped in to save the impecunious poet from the debtors' prison.

The ultra-modern bar in the recently refurbished Rummer.

The original part of the inn is accessed down All Saints' Lane – a narrow passage leading from Corn Street to the heart of the old Flower Market. The present inn has been known as the Rummer (a large drinking vessel for rum) for over two hundred years but its history goes back to 1241 when it was called The Greene Lattis and granted Bristol's first licence.

The name and ownership have changed many times over the centuries. The early premises were rebuilt in 1440 but the name and present structure was finally fixed in 1743 and in 1784 it became Bristol's first coaching inn. Today's interior has been stripped to clean simple lines but there are still some signs of antiquity to be found if you look carefully.

This quiet sixteen-bedroom country town hotel dates back to 1452 and is built of stones from the nearby Norman Castle.

CASTLE CARY
George Inn
Parson James Woodforde (1740 - 1803)

The small market town of Castle Cary has now absorbed the neighbouring village of Ansford which stands on the old coaching route from Poole to Bristol. James Woodforde was born at the Parsonage in Ansford on 27 June 1740. In adulthood he led an uneventful, unambitious life as a clergyman: a life unremarkable but for one thing - for nearly 45 years he kept a diary which provides a unique insight into the everyday routines and concerns of eighteenth-century rural England.

For a decade from 1763 he worked here as a curate and his diary entries at this time are thickly peopled with memorable Somerset characters from all strata of society, many of them immortalised with nick-names including: Peter 'Cherry Ripe' Coles, 'Mumper' Clarke and 'Riddle' Tucker. The George Inn

Above: The elm beam above this inglenook was growing as a young tree in AD 900.
Below: The attractive dining room with its pleasing blend of furnishing styles.

in the centre of Castle Cary features prominently. The entry for 1 March 1768 records the happenings at election time:

> *Great dinners etc., given today at the George Inn. There were a great multitude of all sorts, gentle and simple. Bells ringing etc., and a great procession through Town with Musick playing and guns firing.*

And less happy occasions like that of 2 July 1777 when a crowd assembled at the George to see the wretched Robert Biggins lashed to a cart and whipped round the streets of the town for stealing potatoes. There was a collection of seventeen shillings and six pence for the Hangman 'an old man and most villainous looking' who did the whipping but James Woodforde would have none of it.

DUNSTER
Luttrell Arms
Thomas Hardy (1840 - 1928)

The Luttrell Arms at Dunster features as the Lord-Quantock-Arms at Markton in Thomas Hardy's novel *A Laodicean*.

Set in a commanding position at one end of Dunster's only street is the Castle and at the other end is the Luttrell Arms – used in medieval times as a guest house by the Abbots of Cleeve. The core of the hotel is a fifteenth-century Gothic Hall which is now divided by a floor into two parts. The upper chamber contains a fine hammer-beam roof and the lower chamber, which was once the inn kitchen is now the bar. The porch tower was built between 1622 and 1629.

The first half of Thomas Hardy's novel *A Laodicean* centres around Dunster and most of the action takes place in Stancy Castle and two local inns. The principal of these is the Lord-Quantock-Arms at Markton which is easily recognisable as the Luttrell Arms.

George Somerset is an architect who has come to work on the castle inherited by Paula Power from her railway-magnet father. Written when Hardy was on the threshold of middle age, the novel draws deeply on early personal sources and he admitted it: 'contained more of the facts of his own life than anything he had written'.

An example of the fine plasterwork which dates from 1651.

The building is known to have been an inn called the Ship in 1651 and some of the rooms have fine plasterwork dating

The inn began life as a guest house of the Abbots of Cleeve whose ruined Cistercian monastery is about 4 miles distant.

from that time. It became the Luttrell Arms in 1799 in compliment to Hugh Luttrell whose family had been lords of the manor since 1404. The inn and restaurant are stylish and comfortable. For a more informal experience, the bar is a traditional English pub and has a summer garden terrace.

The upper chamber of the original Gothic Hall contains a fine hammer-beam roof, part of which is seen here in one of the bedrooms.

FRESHFORD
The Inn
Peter Lovesey (1936 -)

The Inn at Freshford enjoys one of the most attractive of settings on the banks of the River Frome.

Among his numerous successful historical and contemporary stories Peter Lovesey has written a dozen Somerset-based crime novels featuring modern-day Bath police detective Peter Diamond. The books are peppered with local pubs, too many for me to cover them all. If you haven't read one of Lovesey's thrillers you might like to try *The Secret Hangman* (2007). It features the George at Norton St Philip, the Hadley Arms at Combe Down and The Inn here at Freshford.

This sixteenth-century stone-built inn enjoys one of the loveliest settings on the banks of the River Frome near it's confluence with the Avon. Diamond and attractive novice detective Ingeborg have traced a man they want to interview to an address in Freshford village but unfortunately he is not at home. At this point Diamond has a hunch, and tells Ingeborg that someone at the inn might have some information.

The George at Norton St Philip: 'a mighty and magnificent pub'.

What he didn't tell her was that his hunches rarely amounted to anything. His real purpose in going in was a late lunch of

89

fish and chips. The landlord said Danny came in sometimes, but never stayed long. He'd take his drink and a packet of crisps to an empty table. He usually had a paper with him and did the crossword. Afterwards they took their drinks outside and sat on the wall of the packhorse bridge listening to the ripple and gurgle of the Avon. Across a green field, the steep side of the Limpley Stoke Valley was covered in lush foliage. 'Not bad, eh?' he said. 'Better than watching your friend Dr Sealy doing a post-mortem.'

Later in the story Diamond goes to the George at Norton St Philip in pursuit of information:

'Do you know the George' Leaman nodded. 'Everyone who has been to Norton knows the George Inn, a mighty and magnificent pub said to have been built by the monks of Hinton Charterhouse. Samuel Pepys, Oliver Cromwell and the Duke of Monmouth stayed there, although not at the same time or Pepys' Diary might have had an interesting entry'. 'He's waiting for us in the main bar,' Diamond said. 'Off school with stress and he goes to the pub?'

The thrilling climax of *The Secret Hangman* begins with a search of the labyrinths created by the excavation of Bath stone. The tunnels were accessed at the time from the garden of the Hadley Arms at Combe Down.

The George & Pilgrims featues in J. C. Powys' tour-de-force novel *A Glastonbury Romance*.

GLASTONBURY
George & Pilgrims
John Cowper Powys (1872 - 1963)

Tom Barter is one of the main characters in John Cowper Powys' 1932 tour-de-force *A Glastonbury Romance*. He has rooms in Glastonbury High Street next to the George & Pilgrims and enjoys spending time in this very special old inn.

> *His diurnal relaxation was his mid-day dinner at the Pilgrims, which he relished with the appetite of a fox-hunter. The waitresses there, with every one of whom, especially with a girl called Clarissa Smith, he had a separate and complete*

Above: Horses used to go through this passage to access the yard and stables.

Below: The interior reflects the tradition of one of the finest surviving medieval inns in Britain.

understanding, rivaled each other in catering to his taste. Tom's taste was all for freshly cooked meats and substantial puddings. Any petticoat fluttering about these solid viands was sauce enough for him.

Powys has been described as a powerful genius and this work – which has been compared with the fictions of Tolstoy and Dostoevsky – is his masterpiece. It is a novel on a huge scale in which the small town of Glastonbury and its legends, both Christian and pagan, exert a supernatural influence on

the life and the complex loves – both sacred and sexual – of the inhabitants.

The George and Pilgrims Inn was built by Abbot Selwood around 1465 and replaced an earlier inn on the site. The 'Pilgrims' part of the name acknowledges that it was built to accommodate visitors who flocked to the abbey and it remains as one of the finest surviving medieval inns in Britain. The ancient building would not look out of place among the Oxford colleges.

The sign depicts a Crusader knight prepared to defend pilgrims.

Although only eleven metres wide, viewed from the opposite side of the narrow high street it looks twice the size. In the front bar, the mullioned windows with their carved stone surrounds look out on to the modern street scene but the interior furnishings are genuinely antique and iron gates can still close off the cosy, pubby bar as they have done for centuries.

The Rifleman's Arms at 4 Chilkwell Street, features as St Michael's Inn in J. C. Powys' powerful novel *A Glastonbury Romance*.

GLASTONBURY
Rifleman's Arms
John Cowper Powys (1872 - 1963)

Six pubs feature in John Cowper Powys's powerful novel *A Glastonbury Romance* and three of them are in Glastonbury itself. The George & Pilgrims is described in the previous entry, Dickery's, now demolished, stood in the former cattle market and St Michael's Inn can be identified as the seventeenth-century Rifleman's Arms at number 4 Chilkwell Street, where licensing laws were liberally interpreted:

> *The present dictators of Glastonbury would of a surety never have dared officially to interfere with the national regulations about the closing hours of public houses, but once the local police-force had received a hint in favour of greater laxity from the mayor of the town, it became easy for the smaller taverns, like St Michael's on Chilkwell Street, and Dickery's*

at the Cattle Market, to admit a group of habitual customers,
while keeping their blinds down and shutters closed.

The Rifleman is unfussy and the dim lighting and low ceilings
help convey the very real impres-
sion of antiquity. Entering
through the central door, the original two small rooms on either
side have been combined to form
the bar. A central doorway from
the bar leads through to a small
parlour which features significantly in the story.

In the brick fireplace is an old

kitchen range and above the mantle-shelf are a couple of
framed sepia photographs. One is of Edgar Masters, a former
owner of the Rifleman's Arms who died in 1883 aged 79. The

The original two small
front rooms have
been combined to
form the bar.

other is of his wife Matilda who died
the same year aged 68 – both are
buried in Glastonbury cemetery.
Beyond the parlour is a brightly-lit
modern dining room extension, a
good games room and a sunny
terrace.

The old kitchen range in the parlour with the photographs of the landlord and his wife in the mid eighteen
hundreds.

Virginia Woolf and her husband Leonard honeymooned here in 1912.

HOLFORD
Plough
Virginia Woolf (1882 - 1941)

In 1912, Virginia Woolf and her husband Leonard honeymooned here in this seventeenth-century pub. On a postcard sent to her friend Lytton Strachey Virginia wrote: 'Divine country, literary associations, cream for every meal.'

The following year Virginia was suffering from one of her recurring bouts of mental illness and, following medical advice, the couple took a holiday and chose to revisit the pub. In his autobiography Leonard writes of the Plough:

> *The people who kept it were pure Holford folk. The food was delicious. Nothing could be better than the bread, butter, cream and eggs and bacon of the Somersetshire breakfast with which you begin your morning.*

But in his diary Leonard recorded Virginia's mood swings: 'bad mornings and good evenings, delusions by day and peaceful nights, bad nights and cheerful days.' Increasingly concerned, he telegraphed for their friend Ka Cox to join them; she arrived the next day, 2 September. Despite her arrival Virginia was no better and, during the return journey to London six days later, Leonard had to restrain his wife from jumping from the train.

'Exmoor Ale' natrurally takes pride of place in the Plough's bar.

In the village bar is an atmospheric painting of the pub as Virginia and Leonard would have known it in quieter days when the road outside was an unmade single carriageway.

Two dining rooms lead off from the bar, the smaller of which has an inglenook and a mass of carved Tudor beams.

The Rose & Crown, Huish Episcopi is featured in Ian Marchant's *The Longest Crawl*.

Rose & Crown (Eli's)

Ian Marchant (1958 -)

Ian Marchant is a novelist, short story writer, dramatist, travel writer and an occasional presenter for BBC Radio Four. Simon Armitage has described Marchant's latest travel memoir *The Longest Crawl* as: 'Drunkenly funny, obsessively factual, soberingly poignant'.

The standing-room-only taproom

The Longest Crawl takes its underlying theme from G.K. Chesterton's poem *The Rolling English Road*. Ian and his photographer friend Perry Venus determined to go on the longest pub crawl possible in the British Isles from the Scilly Isles to Shetland. Almost from the start, they were advised by people they met: 'If you get the chance, you should go to Eli's in Huish Episcopi'.

Eileen Pittard's family have been running this very unspoilt thatched pub for well over 140 years and now her son and two daughters are involved in the business. Known locally as 'Eli's' – after Elijah Scott, grandfather of the present family. This special pub maintains a determinedly unpretentious atmosphere and character. To enter is to take a real step back in time. In his book, Marchant confirms this when he says:

We drove through the village [Huish Episcopi] several times
without spotting Eli's. We asked a Goth girl at a bus stop,

Sam is one of the latest members of the Pittard dynasty to dispense beer in the pub with no bar.

The interior is a series of cottagey style rooms some of which are decorated with family photographs, including those of Eileen's two uncles who were killed in the First World War.

and she put us on the right road. 'It's not really called Eli's' she said. 'Really, it's called the Rose & Crown. Go down there and you can't miss it'.

When they arrived, they were unimpressed with the exterior of the early nineteenth-century pub: 'It was difficult to see why we had been told to come here by so many people. Until we went inside'. People in the know speak of this pub in hallowed terms and, if you get a chance to visit, you will understand why.

The craftsman built gents' urinal constructed from sections of old sewer pipes is located outside across the yard.

The honey-coloured Hamstone inn stands proud above a raised pavement at the top of the town on the old coach road to Exeter.

ILMINSTER

Bell

William Makepeace Thakeray (1811 - 1863)

The Luck of Barry Lyndon is a picaresque novel about a member of the Irish gentry trying to become a member of the English aristocracy. Thackeray based the story on the real life and exploits of the Anglo-Irish rakehell and fortune-hunter Andrew Robinson Stoney. Shortly after his marriage to Honoria the widow of the late Right Honourable Sir Charles Lyndon in May 1773 – the elegant and accomplished Barry Lyndon set out to visit his estates in the West of England, where he had never yet set foot.

He and his Honoria and suite left London in three chariots, each with four horses. An outrider in livery went before and bespoke lodgings from town to town. On the second night they stayed here in the Bell at Ilminster. In chapter seventeen of the novel we are given an insight into Lyndon's honeymoon activities.

> *In our journey westward my Lady Lyndon chose to quarrel with me because I pulled out a pipe of tobacco (the habit of smoking which I had acquired in Germany when a soldier in Billow's, and could never give it over), and smoked it in the carriage; and also her Ladyship chose to take umbrage both at Ilminster and Andover, because in the evenings when we lay there I chose to invite the landlords of the 'Bell' and the 'Lion' to crack a bottle with me.*

By the third day Lady Lyndon was lighting his pipe for him and asking him humbly whether he would not wish the landlady as well as the host to dine with them.

In 1975 Stanley Kubrick made a film based on the novel starring Ryan O'Neil as the eighteenth century Irish adventurer. The movie had a modest commercial success and a mixed critical reception but is now recognized by many, including Barry Norman, as one of Kubrick's finest films.

The bar where, on his honeymoon, Barry Lyndon invited the landlord to crack a bottle with him.

Edward Thomas stayed in this seven-teenth-century former coaching inn in 1913 and wrote about the experience in his prose work *In Pursuit of Spring*.

KILVE

Hood Arms

Edward Thomas (1878 - 1917)

Writer and poet Edward Thomas was killed at the Battle of Arras in 1917. In his prose work *In Pursuit of Spring*, written four years earlier he tells us:

> *I had lunch at the 'Hood Arms', and made up my mind to stay for the night. Kilve, dark and quiet, showed one or two faint lights. Only when I lay in bed did I recognise the two sounds that made the murmurous silence of Kilve – the whisper of its brook, and the bleat of sheep very far off.*

The 'murmurous silence of Kilve' is a thing we can only imagine. Today the pub fronts directly on to the busy A39 but when Thomas stayed here in 1913 the road carried hardly any motor traffic. There are a number of photos in the bar of the pub as it looked in Thomas' time. One of these shows a small chapel attached to the building which belonged to the local friendly society.

Friendly societies were the forerunners of our modern trade unions and were often formed in pubs. The symbol for this Kilve brotherhood was derived from the Coat of Arms of Admiral Hood (1724-1816) – a black Cornish crow (chough) with crossed anchor – and explains the unusual present-day pub sign.

The décor throughout the inn reflects the Exmoor and Quantock passion for fox and stag hunting.

Another of the photos shows the very young landlord and landlady, Frank and Annie Stevens, whom Edward Thomas would have met. They took over the pub in 1909 and stayed for fifty-two years. One of their grand-daughters, Penny Davis, worked here as a girl and was still living in Kilve when I first called.

In 2004 this seventeenth-century former coaching inn under-went a sympathetic renovation. There is now a woodburner in the bar, a cosy little plush lounge and a restaurant. Outside there are tables on sheltered back terrace in a delightful walled garden. Beware; if you stop for lunch at the Hood Arms today, you too might be tempted to make up your mind to stay the night. They have 12 stylish bedrooms including those in their Stag Lodge in the courtyard garden.

The pub sign with the Cornish chough and crossed anchor is a reminder of the local friendly society.

NETHER STOWEY
Rose & Crown

John Taylor - 'The Water Poet' (1578 -1653)

Beginning as a humble Thames Waterman, John Taylor became a Jacobean 'media celebrity'. He was a prolific, colourful and popular writer with an acute observation of men and manners. Through the published accounts of his eccentric walking tours he gives us a unique picture of England from James I to the civil war. When he stayed here in the Rose & Crown in 1649 he found that:

> *The hostess was out of town, mine host was very sufficiently drunk, the house most delicately decked with artificial and natural sluttery.*

Over the years this sixteenth-century former posting inn has undergone extensive renovations. In Victorian times the thatched roof was tiled and slated.

The cosy log-fire bar is decorated with interesting old local photographs. Above the fireplace is a framed account of John Taylor's visit.

On this West Country excursion he tore his breeches on a stile and had them roughly patched at Bridgwater before he 'came to a ragged market town called Neatherstoy'. Having placed his order with the landlord, he sat in the street outside the pub for three hours waiting for his supper; because he could not bear the 'odours and contagious perfume' within. Or the tapestry of spider's webs or the smoke that was 'so palpable and perspicuous' he could 'scarcely see anything else'. Supper was not forthcoming and he went to bed hungry only to be bitten all night by fleas the size of new boiled peas, before being woken at dawn by bawling children, barking curs and hogs crying out for their breakfast: 'so I arose and travelled almost sleeping towards Dunster'.

Today the Rose & Crown is warm, welcoming and friendly. Many interesting features of the pub's historic past are still to be seen, with lots of exposed beams

Built in 1230; the George is arguably England's oldest licensed premises.

NORTON ST PHILIP
George Inn

Samuel Pepys (1633 – 1703)

In the summer of 1668 Samuel Pepys, his wife Elizabeth and their two servants made a brief excursion into the West Country. On 12 of June they left the George Inn in Salisbury heading for Bath and Pepys' diary entry records:

In 1685, following the Battle of Sedgemoor, the corridors of this historic inn were thronged with soldiers.

Up, finding our beds good, but lousy; which made us merry.
We set off led to my great content by our landlord to Philips-
Norton.

At Norton St Philip, Pepys visited the church and wondered
at a tomb of a Knight Templar and one of Siamese twin sisters:
the Fair Maids of Foscott. He also comments on the 'very fine
ring of six bells, and they mighty tuneable'. And he records
dining very well here at the inn for 10s before moving on
before nightfall to Bath.

Samuel Pepys aside, the George is best remembered for the
part it played in the Monmouth Rebellion. First providing the
headquarters for the Duke and his men and, after their defeat
at the Battle of Sedgemoor in 1685, acting as the Court of
Retribution for Judge Jeffreys who hanged 12 men here at the
crossroads.

The galleried
bedrooms are still in
use.

Built of local brown stone with jetted timber-framed first and second floors, the George began life in 1230 as a guest house for Hinton Priory. It was purpose built to accommodate travellers and merchants coming to the annual wool fairs that were held in the village from the late thirteenth century until 1902.

After the Dissolution of the Monasteries in 1539 it became an inn. By the later part of the seventeenth century the George had thirty-five beds and stabling for ninety horses. In the eighteenth century the prosperity of the village declined but the coaching route to Bath ensured the inn continued to flourish.

This wonderful old building has been offering hospitality to travellers for over 700 years.

OAKHILL
Oakhill Inn
Edward Thomas (1878 - 1917)

In 1913, the poet Edward Thomas undertook a cycling tour of North Somerset writing of his experience in *In Pursuit of Spring*. He describes the people and landscapes of Southern England in the last months before the First World War. Journeying from Nettlebridge up the northern slope of the Mendips he recalls a former visit to Oakhill and its inn:

> *The 'Oak Hill' inn, a good inn, hangs out its name on a horizontal bar, ending in a gilded oak leaf and acorn. I had lunch there once of the best possible fat bacon and bread fried in the fat, for a shilling; and for nothing, the company of a citizen of Wells, a hearty, strong-voiced man, who read the* Standard *over a beef-steak, a pint of cider, and a good deal of cheese, and at intervals instructed me on the roads of the Mendips, the scenery, the celebrated places, and also praised his city and praised the stout of Oak Hill. Then he smacked his lips, pressed his bowler tight down on his head, and drove off towards Leigh upon Mendip.*

The solid stone-built Oakhill Inn stands on the corner of Bath Road and Fosse Road.

The inn signage has been updated but the 'horizontal bar, ending in a gilded oak leaf and acorn' is still there.

The earliest date recorded for the inn is 29 September 1773 on a deed of release from Mrs Mary James to Mesers Jordon and Perkins. In the centre of the village is the original Oakhill

Brewery building (now apartments) dating from 1769 and once famous for the stout – praised by the hearty man. An advertisement of the time promotes their 'Double Stout Invalid Porter'.

Many of the period features remain from Edward Thomas' time.

PORLOCK
The Ship
Robert Southey (1774 - 1843)

The Ship Inn is one of the oldest inns on Exmoor.

In 1799, Robert and Edith Southey set off from Bristol for a tour of the Exmoor coast, arranging to return via Nether Stowey to stay with Samuel Coleridge. Unfortunately Edith became ill at Minehead, and Southey undertook a number of excursions on his own. On 8 August he was driven to Porlock by John Cruickshank, a friend and neighbour of Coleridge. In a letter to his brother Southey wrote:

Tom, you have talked of Somersetshire and its beauties but you have never seen the finest part. The neighbourhood of Stowey, Minehead and Porlock exceed anything I have seen in England before…

That evening he lodged here at the Ship Inn, where:

> *the bedroom reminded me of Spain, two long old dark tables*
> *with benches and an old chest composed its furniture: but*
> *there was an oval looking-glass, a decent pot de chambre and*
> *no fleas.*

The next day was chilly and wet and he stayed by the inn fire in a nook now known as 'Southey's Corner' and composed his sonnet *To Porlock* which includes the lines:

> *Here by the summer rain confined;*
> *but often shall hereafter call to mind*
> *How here, a patient prisoner 'twas my lot*
> *To wear the lonely, lingering close of day,*
> *Making my sonnet by the ale house fire,*
> *Whilst Idleness and Solitude inspire*
> *Dull rhymes to pass the duller hours away.*

A week later this 'Dull rhyme' brought him a guinea from the *Morning Post*. In 1813 he was made Poet Laureate.

Dating to the thirteenth century, the Ship Inn is one of the oldest inns on Exmoor, with roaring log fires in the winter and a large outdoor seating area and children's play area for the summer months. The inn's excellent website gives a full history of this special place.

The Ship's dining room is decorated with interesting old photographs of Porlock and Exmoor.

WATCHET
Bell Inn
Samuel Taylor Coleridge (1772 – 1834)

In the autumn of 1797 Samuel Taylor Coleridge walked over the Quantock Hills from his home in Nether Stowey, to link up with his friends William and Dorothy Wordsworth. His intention was to join them on a walking tour of the North Somerst coast. Wordsworth later recalled:

> *Coleridge, my sister and myself started from Alfoxden with a view to visit Lynton and the Valley of Stones … In the course of this walk was planned the poem of the* Ancient Mariner.

They agreed that a poem should be published to cover the cost of their journey and felt that the *Monthly Magazine* would pay £5 for a ballad based on the supernatural, a popular subject at the time. The main theme came from a dream of a spectre ship experienced by Coleridge's friend, John Cruikshank. Wordsworth added the idea of the crime of shooting the albatross from reading a book about rounding Cape Horn in a ship. He contributed a few lines to the poem, but soon gave up trying to work with Coleridge.

Below left: Samuel Taylor Coleridge stayed here in the autumn of 1797 with his friends William and Dorothy Wordsworth.

Below right: The first few lines of *The Rime of the Ancient Mariner* were written on the overnight stay at the inn.

The dining room is a mix of modern comfort and original features

On the first night the trio stayed here at the Bell Inn. Watchet Harbour and its setting, including the landmark prominence of the twelfth-century church of St Decuman's, became the inspiration for the point of departure of the Mariner. It is also

the point of his return when he tells the tale of his epic voyage. As a tribute to Coleridge, and his poetic masterpiece, the Watchet Market House Museum Society commissioned a statue of the Ancient Mariner which was erected on the Esplanade in 2003. The family-run sixteenth-century Bell Inn is situated in Market Street, a few yards from the marina.

A 7-foot high effigy of the Mariner, with the albatross tied round his neck, stands on the Esplanade at Watchet Harbour.

The fifteenth-century Crown, stands in the market place adjacent to the grounds of the Bishop's Palace.

WELLS
Crown

Warwick Deeping (1877 -1950)

Between the end of the First World War and his death in 1950, Warwick Deeping wrote more than 60 bestselling novels, a number of which were made into films. His most popular book, *Sorrell and Son* published in 1925, was the subject of a

Subtle lighting, wooden floors and natural stone walls give a stylish feel to the dining room.

successful television adaptation screened on ITV in the 1980s. The story is set in the small Cathedral town of Staunton; easily identified as Wells with descriptions of the Cathedral, the moated Bishops' Palace and the Canons' Houses in Vicars' Close.

Stephen Sorrell, a decorated war hero, raises his son Kit alone after his wife deserts him during the boy's infancy. He travels to Staunton to take up a promising job offer only to find that the man who made him the offer has died. As a result, Sorrell is forced to take menial work as a porter at the Angel Inn, where a large part of the action takes place.

He rose and walked back to the Angel Inn, and turning in at the arched entry, found a doorway on his left that led into a broad passage. He was to learn to know that passage very well, and to hate it and its slippery oil-cloth, and the stairs that went up from it into the darkness. A lounge enlarged itself on the right, the windows looking into the courtyard; and opening from the other side of the lounge were the office, the passage to the kitchen, the 'Cubby Hole', and the back entrance to the 'bar!

As a result of *Hot Fuzz* the Crown is now one of the top 100 Famous Grouse pubs.

In an age when the printed word was the dominant entertainment medium he was at the top of the popular novelist tree and enjoyed the kind of international star status we generally associate today with entertainers or media personalities.

In 2007 the comedy film *Hot Fuzz* was shot in and around the hotel. Stars of the film, Nick Frost and Simon Pegg are seen here with director Edgar Wright (on the right) who co-wrote the screenplay with Pegg.

The Rising Sun where Edward Thomas stopped in the spring of 1913 suffered a disastrous fire in 2002.

WEST BAGBOROUGH
Rising Sun
Edward Thomas (1878 - 1917)

Before he found his true vocation as a poet, Edward Thomas wrote a number of travel books to pay the rent. In 1913, he undertook a cycling tour of North Somerset and wrote of his experience in *In Pursuit of Spring*. After leaving Kilve he cycled out along the road from Williton to Taunton, passing the Carew Arms at Crowcombe:

> *By the time I reached Crowcombe, the sun was bright. This village standing at the entrance to a great cloudy coomb of oaks and pine trees, is a thatched street containing the 'Carew Arms' a long, white inn having a small porch, and over it a signboard bearing a coat of arms and the words J'espere bien.*

In a short while he reached West Bagborough and the Rising Sun:

Rain threatened again, and I went into the inn to eat and see what would happen. Two old men sat in the small settle at the fireside talking of cold weather, for so they deemed it. Bent, grinning old men they were, using rustic, deliberate, grave speech, as they drank their beer and ate a few fancy biscuits. One of them was so old that never in his life had he done a stroke of gardening on a Good Friday; he knew a woman that did so once when he was a lad, and she perished shortly after in great pain.

The Rising Sun dates back to 1573 and, was originally called The Shepherd's Crook but known to the villagers simply as 'Crook'. The same heavy oak front door that Thomas pushed against in 1913 now opens onto a very changed scene. In January 2002 a disastrous fire gutted the beautiful old pub. Within a year, it was refitted and open again for business. All that remains of the original interior are two heavy ceiling beams, too dense to burn quickly and the defiantly solid thick stone walls. The expensive reincarnation is bold, craftsman-led and has been accomplished with great style; incorporating light oak, glass and natural slate floors.

The front section of the Carew Arms at Crowcombe, with its old fashioned bar, remains as Edward Thomas would have known it.

Bear

Parson James Woodforde (1740 - 1803)

Sir Terry Pratchett (1948 -)

Like The Pipers Inn at Ashcott, the Bear Hotel at Wincanton has two Famous Grouse top 100 plaques commemorating its

association with two famous writers. And like The Pipers, one of the writers is the notable diarist Parson James Woodforde. The restaurant tablemats in the Bear celebrate Woodforde's first visit during August 24 and 25 1761 when he recorded in *The Diary of a Country Parson* that his lodgings were very good. He paid 2 shillings and 5p for breakfast, horses etc; and tipped the hostler and the chambermaid 6p each.

On a subsequent visit six years later in 1767, there is a record of him taking a Miss Jordan to a concert and 'a very genteel ball' at the Bear. He tells us that on 16 February he danced

Built in 1720, the section to the left of the front door was later incorporated from an adjoining building.

A bear stands sentinel by one of the log fires in the heavily beamed bar.

Recognition of Parson Woodforde's association with the inn is to be seen on the restaurant placemats and this Famous Grouse plaque.

every dance with Miss Jordan from 10 to 4 in the morning *'the best dancer in the room'*. Woodforde had an uncle called Thomas and the Miss Jordan with whom he danced was the niece of Thomas' wife.

It also appears that James Lintern, the landlord of the Bear at the time, was known to Woodforde. He had formerly been the chaise driver from the Ansford, Woodforde's local inn which is now a private house.

The other Grouse whisky plaque tells us that the Bear is now famous as the meeting place of 'The Discworld Tribe': devoted fans of the series of books by Sir Terry Pratchett. Sir Terry himself often attends the gatherings and conventions at the Bear. The celebrated author has sold more than 55 million books worldwide and has had his works translated into 33 languages.

Wincanton's 'Ankh-Morpork Consulate', up hill from the Bear, is a wonderfully quirky shop dedicated to all things Discworld.

Wincanton was officially twinned in 2002 with the fictional city of 'Ankh-Morpork' from the novels, becoming the first UK town to link with a fictional place. The Kingwell Rise development in the town has streets named Peach Pie Street and Treacle Mine Road etc., named after the comic fantasy series of novels. The Bear is listed in Sir Terry's *Ankh-Morpork City Guide*.

Wincanton suffered several serious fires during the seventeenth century. One great fire in 1707 is believed to have started in the Bear and it destroyed much of town. The present building dates from 1720 when it was purpose built as a coaching inn.

Blackmore stayed in a number of inns around Exmoor, including this one, whilst researching the background for *Lorna Doone*.

Royal Oak

R. D. Blackmore (1825 - 1900)

R. D. Blackmore stayed at or called in to a number of inns around Exmoor whilst researching the background for *Lorna Doone*. In the Royal Oak here at Withypool there is a framed letter dated July 10 1866 written from Blackmore's London home at Teddington. It is addressed to Mr Warner, the land-lord at the time and reads:

It will give me great pleasure to be with you (if possible) at the time you mention. But I am so terribly pressed this week that I cannot be certain of the pleasure.

Lorna Doone is the most famous and celebrated of R. D. Black-

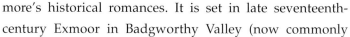

more's historical romances. It is set in late seventeenth-century Exmoor in Badgworthy Valley (now commonly known as 'Doone Valley') where many Blackmore landscapes can still be found. The story is one of romance where a family of outlaws, the Doones, begin to plague the land. Young John Ridd, the hero of the yarn, is only twelve when the book opens and he grows up with the threat of the Doones who have begun to burn farms, attack men and carry off women.

Lorna Doone is the most famous and celebrated of R.D. Blackmore's historical romances.

John grows up to be a man of great stature and power and falls in love with Lorna who he must save from the Doones and from nature itself during a fierce blizzard. It is a near-tragic romance that includes certain historical and legendary figures, including Judge Jeffrys of Bloody Assizes infamy, Tom Fagus (a West Country Robin Hood) and the Doones themselves who are based on actual historical personages.

This lovely, welcoming pub has two softly lit bars with lots of old pots hanging from the beamed ceilings. The lounge bar is the heart of the pub and dates back three hundred years. Here a vast wood fire fills the room with good cheer. Adjacent to this room lie further bars and a beautifully appointed restaurant of a similar antiquity.

This statue of Lorna Doone, outside the Exmoor National Park Rangers office in Dulverton was given to the town in 1990 by American, Dr Whitman Pearson.

The Wookey Hole Inn stands across the lane from Wookey Hole Caves.

WOOKEY HOLE
Wookey Hole Inn
John Cowper Powys (1872 - 1963)

Margaret Drabble declared John Cowper Powys' *A Glastonbury Romance* to be the greatest novel of the twentieth century. In the story, the Wookey Hole Inn is used as the model for the Zoyland Arms, where Mr Lamb the landlord takes a sixpence from tourists visiting the caves.

What more could you ask for from an inn?

The central character is the ruthless hard-nosed industrialist Philip Crow, whose private plane is flown by his manager Tom Barter. They arrive at Crow's private landing strip to inspect his factory and further his ambitions of exploiting the industrial potential of the cave system. His intention is to trample into the dust the pious legends of Glastonbury. The pair have arranged to stay in the Zoyland Arms where they have their own rooms and where other members of the

A conservative corner of this otherwise brightly decorated inn

story's large cast are present. The experience of flying over the Somerset landscape has a profound effect on Crow and when he reached the inn he:

> ...*was still in an unusual state of excitement as he ran upstairs to his little room, where the gas had already been lit. His face at that moment presented a mask of stoney human fanaticism.*

The ground floor of this tall building is constructed of sandstone and on the upper floors black beams contrast with white rendering. Viewed against the backdrop of the steeply rising wooded Mendip Hills, this successful *Les Routiers* Hotel has the air of an Alpine inn. However, befitting the strange area of Glasonbury, the pub's own website describes it as 'funky'.

The quirky pub sign is a beer-glass with a heart, angel's wings and a halo.

The only clue from the exterior that you are about to enter somewhere different is the pub sign – a black outline symbol of a beer-glass with a heart, angel's wings and a halo. In this idiosyncratic, brightly decorated inn the 'heavenly' theme is continued with depictions of angels, and even a cross.

SELECTED BIBLIOGRAPHY

Alisdair Aird & Fiona Stapley, *The Good Pub Guide*

Derry Brabbs, *English Country Pubs*

Ted Bruning, *Historic Inns of England*

Robert M. Cooper, *The Literary Guide and Companion to Southern England*

A. W. Coysh, *Historic English Inns*

Denys Kay Robinson, *The Landscape of Thomas Hardy*

Hermann Lea, *The Hardy Guides*

Rodney Legg, *Literary Dorset*

Ian Merchant, *The Longest Crawl*

B. W. Matz, *Dickensian Inns & Taverns*

B. W. Matz, *The Inns & Taverns of Pickwick*

Andrew Norman, *Enid Blyton & her Enchantment with Dorset*

Peter Tolhurst, *Wessex, A Literary Pilgrimage*